COMPASSIONATE DECLUTTERING

How to Soulfully Surrender Your Stuff

Michelle "Home Coach" Hoff, MA

WISE
INK

BeaN & MOMO,
you two are my family.
DRop the nic!
The years, the years we
have talked about this
have not been wasted.
We have crossed the
finish line ... together.
Thank you! BIGHugs, Bells

ISBN 13: 978-1-63489-521-7

Library of Congress Catalog Number has been applied for.
Printed in the United States of America
First Printing: 2022

26 25 24 23 22   5 4 3 2 1

Cover design by Jason Anscomb
Interior design by Patrick Maloney

Wise Ink Creative Publishing
807 Broadway St. NE
Suite 46
Minneapolis, MN 55413

Contents

For every person struggling to manage excess
and who courageously and tenaciously does.

Introduction

"Life will only change when you become more committed to your dreams than you are to your comfort zone."
BILLY COX

I have an idea I want to share with you.

I want us to tackle the nation's clutter issue as a collective. I see us all holding hands, braver together, facing the mess, each electrified in solidarity to get this stuff under control once and for all. I won't lie to you—this will take work. We'll focus on internal work first to make us stronger, and then the "ass and elbows" kind of work, as my farmer father would say. Needless clutter is sucking the joy out of so many beautiful lives, and I can't take it anymore. I want to help you unleash this burden of excess. Maybe you don't know where in this mess to start, or you're bogged down in the eternal uncertainty of what to do with *it* and the oppressive fear that *it* will come back. Yes, even if *it* gets cleaned up, deep down you believe *it* will get messy again. I promise you I have a plan to ensure this won't be another disastrous attempt at decluttering.

For years, I have been internalizing the plight of my clients and everyone I have ever talked to who has excess, or feels hopeless and overwhelmed. As a graduate in landscape management and horticulture, an owner of a small commercial and residential cleaning business, a designer, a staff member in an integrity-filled creative home furnishings retailer, an interior painter, and a life and home coach, I have over thirty years of experience digging around in people's living spaces. I have a great plan to help you get rid of your stuff once and forever. The genesis of this plan began many years ago as my master's thesis, "Recovering Your Authentic Self Using Home as Your Medium." Hey, this was a self-directed, self-created master's program, and I got to bring anything to the table that would move and improve the human condition. I was an average student in high school and college until grad school, where I managed a (shocking to me) 4.0. I was in the right place at the right time in my life. I was taking only classes I loved. This love thing will come up again.

I love creating home. I come from a long line of home creators. My upholstering, drape- and dress-sewing, dough-beating, bun-making, canning, dinner-party-hosting, doily-slinging grandmother was an impeccable home creator. Stylish, simple, elegant, and approachable with an amazing laugh, she curated her treasures thoughtfully. No excess, just essentials.

Grandma Marie's doctor said her heart, stressed from rheumatic fever, could not take bearing children. In "those days," with fewer options, she pressed on and had six bundles of joy, putting their able butts to work on her 180-acre farm. My mom was the oldest, and when Grandma was worn out or her heart needed a tune-up at the Mayo Clinic, Mom took over, helping to raise her siblings, and managing the home and all the moving parts of a farming family.

As I grew up, Mom set up home in a very similar fashion to Grandma Marie. I have followed in principle as well. Scandinavian blood craves cleanliness, order, and a good time. Work should be fun. I have always loved projects, and I want to make it clear that the decluttering you will embark upon (maybe for the hundredth time) will be productive and fun too.

When I see others struggling to love the space they are in, I want to help. Everyone is closer to creating their loved home than they think. I have pieced together great insights from my family, cleaning clients, design principles, project management experience, life coaching, and therapy (a lot of therapy!) to help others who feel hopelessly buried in stuff create a home that feels like heaven on earth. All you need to do is bring your unique spirit and tenacity, and together with the support of other declutterers, we can clear through the clutter once and for all. Let's free up the excess so you can live the fullest life you have secretly imagined. Can't wait!

Here's what I am thinking. First, we forgive ourselves for the mess. With a tender heart, we surrender to every mistake or failed attempt to clean things up. The energy we spend on trying to tackle excess is exhausting. You have done all you can do. Feeling incomplete after planning, executing, eliminating, organizing, and falling short time after time sucks! So put your arms around yourself.

No, I mean really.

Put your arms around yourself and sincerely, softly forgive yourself. From here on in, you are entering a no-shame zone. Everybody makes mistakes. You are beautiful. You are a warrior. You are courageous. You are a phoenix and you will rise again. It is with this compassion for self that you will succeed in getting rid of excess *forever*.

Compassion for self is the cozy blanket we wrap around ourselves. It's how we heal the cycle of excess and eliminate, excess and eliminate, even if "I have got to declutter!" has only been in your mind. Energy spent in action as well as thought about clutter is still energy wasted if the result is unsatisfying. We have to reengineer a new way of thinking and doing when it comes to excess. What you tried in the past isn't working, so it's time to pave a new pathway, one brick at a time.

You have all the tools needed to lay the foundation for this new path. You are innately creative, resourceful, and whole. This mantra is specific and central to my life coach training. You are not broken. You do not need to be fixed. If you are willing to be curious about how you can get yourself out of this mess, it will happen! This book does not have the answers. *You* have all the know-how already, waiting to be liberated if you're willing to approach this process with curiosity. I am a curious person, so I will bring my curiosity about you during our time here together. This book, your untapped ingenuity, and this community of recovering clutterers are your support as you create this new way of dealing with your mess.

The second piece of work will be to re-parent yourself. Yes, I know this sounds oppressive and hard, but trust me, it will be liberating.

Re-parenting means accepting responsibility for your mess. Admitting you are at the center of your clutter is the first step to recovery. Of course, not all of it is your doing, but the doing that is yours is yours to own. You know this is true or you wouldn't be here. Setting limits and (finally) making the uncomfortable and hard decisions are keys to re-parenting yourself. The many ways in which you have been accumulating or trying to eliminate have to stop. You haven't found the right way to manage this stuff, but that doesn't mean you can't or won't. Stay in the game.

Personal inventory means digging in and understanding what is really important to you. Explore your core personal values, create a vision, and assess the relationship you have with your stuff, all in service of making better decisions on what stays and goes. Be the better, stricter, and more loving parent. Shit's gotta move, right? You have been plugged up long enough. Change what you have been doing, and together let's get 'er done.

Trust yourself and stay curious to some new learning. Here is where hope comes in. The tools you learn in this book will help you prepare the ground, construct the bricks, lay them out, bind them together with mortar, and place them in the new direction facing the bigger life you dream for yourself without masses of stuff pressing down on you. With your path facing a new direction, you can build a fresh and freeing perspective.

What are these bricks? You can learn to be a bolder, kinder, and stronger parent with better boundaries by reconnecting with your truest self through your key core values, which often are buried but sleeping inside your soul. Recover them, and another brick is laid. Your vision for the home you've always wanted will be crystalized. And another brick is laid. Seeing your love shack in your mind's eye becomes the compass you will use to stay focused.

These two tools—personal values and vision—are the power strainer that will sift the crap from the keeper stuff. Use them to strengthen every fiber in your being so you can begin to make stalled decisions and grind through that crammed closet with new clarity. This goes, this goes, this goes, this one must stay. In short order, you will be making clearer decisions, and instead of looking back, you'll be looking forward to new order, with limitless possibilities on the horizon.

Reconstructing your relationship with yourself and your stuff is paramount because the marketing machines of the world will always be hurling things your way even when you are not looking. Learn to hone your peripheral vision and recognize the scent in the air of a shopping frenzy. Strengthen your armor and deflect this machine so you can stay on your path.

The third foundation-building tool will be to turn you into a hard-hat-wearing project manager—pencil, plan, clipboard, and all. Project management is the "ass and elbows" work of decluttering. The key element here is the plan—*your* plan, which I will help you develop skills to create. This plan will tackle any mess you have. Once learned, these skills can't be unlearned. Teaching a person to fish as opposed to bringing them fish is like hiring an organizer versus learning to declutter your own mess. Learning these skills yourself assures lifelong success.

If the whole house has to be tackled, you will break it down into bite-sized pieces, building a priority list one dresser, closet, under-the-bed, or room at a time. Take control. In doing so, overwhelm, the decluttering devil, is defeated. This devil's offspring—fear, defeat, and hopelessness—always tag along too, don't they? Nope. Won't have it. Don't want it. No thank you. Your priorities will keep your eye on the prize to press on.

As a project manager, you will learn how to take things apart, dismantling and dispersing stuff out the door or into the right place according to your vision. Every project manager is different, and you will develop your own style of decluttering. I am not going to tell you how to do this because I am not you. You got yourself into this mess, and you can and will get yourself out of it. This book will give you the means to believe in yourself, to make meaningful choices with planful execution in your own way.

But don't worry. You won't be doing it alone. Clutter doesn't just create piles of stuff; it builds walls of isolation. Reach out to friends who are struggling with managing excess. Share ideas, setbacks, and inspiration in order to rework a plan and press on. Together with our community of clutter-free warriors, we celebrate your wins as a collective!

The fourth and final piece is the decluttering itself and holding yourself accountable to the work of shit shoveling. Accountability is like a mini fire under your butt at all times. This fire, warm and fierce, needs you to keep moving, experimenting, falling, and getting back up in this process of letting go. No one can maintain your momentum but you. Set goals. Do the work. Make progress. Break old habits. Invent new solutions. Revise, then keep moving.

Each chapter of this book will firm up your internal scaffolding to do the heavy lifting. Self-compassion forged by resilience will give you the ability to press through obstacles better than ever before. It makes you ready to face the first pile, cabinet, drawer, storage room, or dining room table, mobilized with a fortified soul and your capable arms and legs. Let's get to work. Tackling one thing at a time. Marching toward your clutter-free vision.

Still, don't kid yourself, and I won't sugarcoat it. This is work. Decluttering takes time. I assure you, getting rid of excess doesn't take nearly as long as it took to amass. Rarely do plans run according to plan. When your plan fails or you fail the plan, rework it. Dig into your creativity and try something new. Pivot when roadblocks and potholes slow you down. Continue to hold yourself in check. Are you on the right path? Does the vision feel real? Don't look to someone else's path—keep your focus on your own unique journey. Review the tools you've learned and remind yourself of *your* values and vision power packs fueling you during this difficult process. Reconnect with these homing tools, connect with your clutter clan network, revise, and above all, keep believing. Press on.

I want you on this journey only if you want to be here. Chuck this book if you are not ready. If you are 1 percent willing, that is enough. In this book you will find some tried-and-true decluttering tips, as well as some new ideas, activities, exercises, questions, and challenges to get this rusty machine moving. Remember, *you* are designing the path, not me. I can't wait to see what you come up with. Your home is calling and it wants you back.

The four key concepts in this book are the tools you will need to get rid of today's excess and avoid the excess of the next day, and the next. Forever. This is not a fad decluttering diet. This is a change in lifestyle.

This working journal is both. Work. A journal. As you make your way through, read. Absorb. Underline ideas that resonate or rattle an old belief. Write notes in the margin or in a separate notebook. Keep track of your hopes, fears, or secrets. Anything that makes you look at your situation in a new way is good. Each chapter contains questions and actions. Participate. Play. Explore. Reunite with your heart in the first several chapters. My wish, and the book's design, is to make you into an Olympic athlete. By the end of the book, you will be in peak shape to actually dig in to your clutter. Feel the fortification that comes from self-love, compassion, distinct values, and vision.

Let's do this together.
I promise, you will get home safely.
I am holding your hand.
Let's get at it!

♪

"Lean on Me"
Bill Withers

1 | Compassion

"If you want others to be happy, practice compassion.
If you want to be happy, practice compassion."
DALAI LAMA

ompassion is a mighty yet soft word, an emotion and an action. Familiar on its edges, warm and caring like the best of our society. Compassion is visible in simple acts of kindness. I am often moved to tears when I see people feeding children, feeding themselves. Strangers opening doors for someone struggling with babies and bags. Kindly mowing an elderly person's lawn. Dropping off gently used clothing to a women's shelter. Tending to those essential needs highlights our vulnerability. Compassion means seeing a need, feeling empathy, and *doing* something to address the ache. All of humanity benefits from giving and receiving these gestures of soul-filling compassion.

Compassion and empathy are often linked but are quite different. Empathy is the ability to feel what another person is feeling. Compassion is empathy plus action. Compassion is kinesthetic; it's doing, giving, or both in order to comfort or lessen pain. Donating money, goods, or time is caring in action. It's compassion.

As neuroscientist Tania Singer reported in 2013, in the journal *Social and Cognitive Neuroscience*, compassion stimulates brain circuits for pleasure and good feeling. Singer further added, "A daily practice of minutes spent cultivating an attitude of compassion strengthens all this wiring." It feels good to

COMPASSION – CARE IN ACTION

live with a compassionate mindset. Emma Seppala, PhD and author of *The Happiness Track,* emphasizes the more compassion you experience, the more tolerance for discomfort is built. Creating and expanding a reservoir of resilience from discomfort is possible and necessary, especially when it comes to decluttering.

Resilience expands when you linger longer in discomfort, feel difficult feelings, and finally make hard decisions. Resilience grows grit. Grit is the ability to do these hard things consistently over an extended period of time. Every decision empowers you to keep making more and more decisions easier and faster. This gritty tenacity will pull fellow declutterers out of paralysis to move from mess to less.

Making all these delayed decisions is hard but rewarding. Dr. Seppala says you will cultivate qualities of compassion—resilience, patience, wisdom, kindness, and, I add, determination to build more stamina to work through bigger and bigger messes. I know a bit about resilience and grit. This book has taken me over a dozen years to write (and rewrite a dozen times). I wanted to give up so many times. What kept me moving was a belief that there might be one person who would be helped from something I had to offer. I would decide again and again that I was in this for the long haul. I wanted to see this to completion. I gave up caring about how long this would take and focused on the finish line.

My home state of Minnesota has the second highest volunteerism rate in the US, next to Utah (2018). The Twin Cities (Minneapolis, St. Paul, and surrounding suburbs) as a metropolitan city are number one in volunteerism as noted by Michelle Griffith in a 2020 *Star Tribune* article. Griffith reports, "Whether it's lending neighbors extra rolls of toilet paper, offering free babysitting or making bagged lunches for those in need, Minnesotans have a reputation for putting others' needs first." As a lifelong Minnesotan, I can say compassion is encouraged and evident on a daily basis.

Full disclosure, Minnesotans aren't perfect. We like our comfort zone which means we like to hang with people we know. We are slow to embrace strangers in our tight-knit family and friend groups. I admit, my own family fit that bill. My daughter attended a French immersion elementary school. Each year, college-aged French interns came to our state, and the elementary school families were asked to host an intern (given space and interest) sometime during the six years our children attended the school.

We had the space. I knew we needed to host. Our only child was a big fan of the idea. But honestly, the thought made my wife and me bristle. *Live* with us?! For five months?! What about our perfectly managed routines of laundry, general lounging, travel, evening TV, and chips? What were the four of us supposed to do together? As the primary orchestrator of our lives, I questioned if we had the bandwidth to give additional time and attention to another person. Eventually, we heeded the call and volunteered to host. A reluctant act of compassion is still compassion.

The interns shared their ten-month stay between two families. Five months with family one, and five months with family two. We were family two. This transition, they warned us, could be difficult, especially when the interns formed a great bond with their first American family, and because a cold Minnesota move in January isn't fun. Naomi, our exotic, blue-haired French intern, arrived and set up home in our unused, lower-level guest room. Within a few days, she was in tears. Her boyfriend back in France had broken up with her. Naomi missed her family *and* her first host family, with whom she grew very close. We jumped in, hugging this sweet stranger as she shared her tears and pain. My wife and I knew this pain. We had been there too. The hurt was real. Life would get better, we told her. She deserved better. Right then and there, our skeptical hearts dissolved. That initial resistance was forgotten as our capacity to love and care for this new person expanded.

Naomi didn't need much. She was already a strong, confident, and capable twenty-two-year-old. As she began to surface from her room, we learned about her amazing French Algerian mom, her father, who was born in France but raised by Indian parents from a French colony (Pondicherry) in India, her smart sister, and her sassy cat, Gatsby. Naomi shared with us her wild taste in music, food she loved and missed, and about the book she was writing. Our type A family slowly relaxed. A lot. Through the power of compassion, Naomi peeled open our hearts and minds in a way that changed us forever.

Compassion opens locked doors. My daughter is an animal whisperer. Having little to no experience with family pets, I had little empathy for pet owners. I couldn't see the value a pet brought to the party. In my mind, pets were an inconvenient responsibility, spontaneity killer, and mess maker. Plus, I swore I would never pick up poop. Ever. "Never getting a pet!" was the clear line drawn in the sand.

After Naomi went back to France, we got a puppy. Willing to be uncomfortable made me more comfortable with the next unknown. What I see now in Miles the dog is pure sweetness, gentle vulnerability, and total love. I care deeply about his well-being and want him to feel big-time doggy joy. Compassion for him has softened me even more. I was personally stretched with Naomi and Miles. They were not the issue—the resistance was within me. Facing resistance increased my resilience.

Hey, no one likes to be uncomfortable, stressed, or challenged. The pain of getting rid of excess sounds daunting and isolating, but you'll never get rid of excess if you don't step up. If you are tired of carrying the weight of excess, build tolerance for discomfort and you will get through the rumbly, rocky decluttering road ahead. There is no way around it but through it.

Self-Compassion: A Muscle

Before we can practice compassion for others, we must first practice self-compassion. The Dalai Lama teaches that compassion is innate and can be strengthened like a muscle. In this case, we're not trying to build your biceps or quadriceps, but the soulful muscles of resilience, patience, wisdom, kindness, and determination.

You can learn to work harder, smarter, and with more compassion—specifically self-compassion. As the airlines say, "Before assisting others with a mask, put yours on first."

If I know you, you have a proven track record of being compassionate to others. Seeing and feeling so much need comes naturally, making it easier to give to others first. In this working journal, you have permission to put yourself at the top of the list. Devote time to healing, knowing, and loving yourself. You and your loving soul are vital to constructing and completing a successful clutter management plan. Here, every word and action asked of you is written to nourish your spirit. Revive the warrior within. Embolden your soul. It's all in service of getting rid of excess for good.

How to Grow Self-Compassion

We can be tough on ourselves. We are judging and critical when we pass a mirror, say the wrong thing in a work meeting, or ruin dinner. Critical messages we tell ourselves fly by without us even noticing. This doesn't mean we don't feel them inside. You can't get through this mess without loving yourself. Grow compassion for yourself through loving patience and kindness, appreciate your earned wisdom, and discover how determined you can be.

Every time you touch this book, I hope you feel your brilliance. Know you are perfect. You are not broken. You do not need to be fixed. Just loved.

Compassion from Patience

I love yoga. Every class, I learn new ways to patiently honor my body, breathe, and hold a posture because yoga is a practice. Patience, too, is a practice. A learning, honoring, and growing patience kind of practice. Stress, anxiety, and depression are commonly associated with clutter, because decluttering can be frustrating. You'll do the wrong thing, get rid of the wrong thing, and focus on the wrong thing. You can count on it. These screwups don't mean you throw in the towel. Temper mistakes and messes with patience, one drawer, box, or closet at a time.

Patience, or a sense of calm, is often hard to access when staring at messes. Both yoga and meditation use breathing to instill a sense of calm and reduce stress and blood pressure. That calm tranquility is the birthplace of patience. If at any time in life—decluttering or otherwise—you're having trouble reaching this state, try doing what is called "box breathing" or four-square breathing:

Step 1: Close your eyes. Breathe in to the count of four.

Step 2: Hold this breath to the count of four.

Step 3: Release all the air from your lungs to the count of four.

Step 4: Count to four before inhaling again.

Breath practice has been proven to instill a meditative state. No tools. No postures. No music. Just you and your breath. Stress, anxiety, and depression

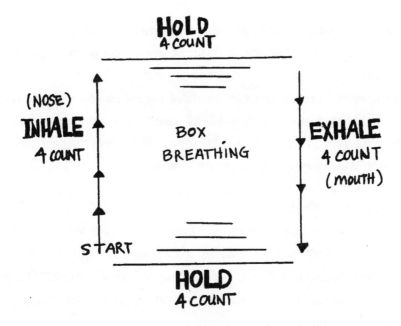

are commonly associated with clutter. While brushing your hair, walking the dog, or waiting in line, set a goal to box breathe five times today, every day. Close your eyes. Add a mantra to repeat at each step.

"I am calm."

"I am patient."

"Everything is OK."

A cycle of five box breaths is the start to bringing calm, and therefore patience.

The need for patience comes with awareness and must be practiced. I am a type A person. As a mom, I know I am not the most patient member of the pack (just ask my daughter), but I do take notice of gifted patient parents with young and challenging children. These parents soothe and artfully tease out the underlying tender feelings of sadness, shame, anger, and loss that cause a kid to act out. Kids and adults both find compassion through patience, and if you can find it in you to be patient with your kids, you can turn that same patience inward. Practice being that patient parent to yourself. Life will interrupt decluttering. Plans of attack will fall apart. How you bounce back from the obstacles without crashing and burning builds strength. That seed of self-compassion will grow one deep breath at a time.

Compassion from Kindness

Both humans and animals instinctively protect and care for those more vulnerable because that is what ensures the survival of the species. Although he was falsely credited with the phrase "survival of the fittest," Darwin was actually a proponent of "survival of the kindest," and called compassion an "almost ever-present instinct."

A kindness mindset means that failure in the past—in this case, when it comes to decluttering—is not a prediction of the future. New actions sprout new possibilities. There will be a Goldilocks of decisions made: some wrong, some so-so, and some you will nail. You are a courageous learner who is being stretched and trying new things. Be easy on your beautiful spirit. With a kind heart, forgive your mistakes. In doing so, you will gather endurance and be able to press on. You can handle more than you think when leading with kindness.

We're lighting a pathway toward a home that functions well and looks, moves, smells, feels, and operates in a way that is 100 percent you. Doing this with kindness renders a home that is that much sweeter.

"Knowing yourself is the beginning of all wisdom."
ARISTOTLE

Compassion from Wisdom

Decluttering forces a personal awakening. You have to look at your behaviors and patterns. Which of your habits have caused these piles? What sneaky ways have you used to avoid projects? What clever tactics have you employed in the past that have worked? When has a decision you made been perfect? Own the excuses you make when things get hard, and mine them for successes. What happened in the past with decluttering will happen again. Become a nonjudgmental observer. Use the wisdom from your epic failures to do something different. Discover what a clever and creative problem solver you are. The best advice I got from my mom buddy Sarah was, "Stay creative!" The same is true for decluttering. If A fails, try B, and if that fails, then give C a shot. Repeat. This wisdom *will* pay off.

Stop sidestepping hard things. Stay in the ring with yourself. Messes *have* to be handled differently if you're going to get out from under this stuff. The definition of insanity is continuing to do the same thing and expecting different results. You're not insane, just scared. Everything is going to be all right. You are so much smarter than you think. The wisdom that you extract from learning is not punishment; it is empowering, and if you let it, it will fuel your determination.

Compassion from Determination

Determination means always moving forward to do better next time. To course correct and find new solutions. Roadblock. Pivot. Speed bump. Slow down. Steep hill. Low gear. Every project presents issues. Open the garage. Get rid of those old skis. Your go-to donation center won't take them. That's a speed bump. So pivot. Place them on the curb or post them on a neighborhood site for "FREE." At the end of the day, the vagrant stuff will have a new home. Determination demonstrated. Drop the mic.

Set a date two weeks out to get rid of a dresser. Communicate with family and friends. Date set. Maybe it goes as planned. Or maybe no one can pick it up or no one wants it. Don't slam on the brakes when you see that road-block. Turn left at the intersection instead. Call a local charity and arrange for them to pick it up ASAP. The trick is to stay loose and keep seeking solutions to the problem at hand. "Easy" happens when you adopt a less rigid approach to decluttering. Getting rid of stuff may not happen the way you expected, but if it goes away, does it matter how? Look at the resilience this determination is teaching you. Get comfortable with your ingenious mind as it proposes fresh ideas and, in doing so, expands your inner toughness.

Right now, the road map to your decluttering plan is in a dark room. The tenets of compassion developed in each chapter will direct you to the matches you'll need to light the candle, locate the string, and turn on the overhead light to find the pen and paper where you will develop your plan to get rid of excess. Patience. Kindness. Wisdom. Determination. Oh my! Along the way, I will sprinkle in pointed questions, accountability, activities, values, vision work, and project management skill building. These tools will give you the grit to work your decluttering plan. You'll get stuff moving out the door with tenderness, not torture.

Engage

Finding motivation to get rid of excess is key, similar to losing weight. From my experience, I know there is one question that hits home every time, and decluttering demands the same question: "What will happen to your life as a result of losing weight?" Besides health, we're often compelled to lose weight for other reasons, like sleeping better, more confidence, less pain from inflammation, or better-fitting clothes.

Getting those outcomes requires daily, persistent decision-making. Decluttering—or trimming excess weight in your home—requires the same dedication.

Every choice you make needs to be made with future benefits in mind. So, what will happen to your life as a result of decluttering? The obvious benefits might be fearless and shame-free entertaining, or an easier time finding your belongings. But go deeper. Make the reasons personal, compelling, and clear. The following exercise allows you to explore your motivation to declutter. When you've lost the will to continue, it is these words that will keep you on course.

Warm-Up Exercise

WHAT: Imagine you are standing in your fully decluttered future space. How will having this decluttered space change your life?

WHY: These reasons will serve as the motivation, catalyst, incentive, and inspiration for doing the decluttering work to come and forever managing your clutter.

TOOLS: One sheet of paper and a writing utensil, computer or tablet.

TASK: Write down three ways life will change as a result of decluttering.

TIME: Thirty minutes.

This exercise is important because what you believe can *become* true and possible. Practice believing you deserve to live in a loved home. Train. Tone the muscles of patience and kindness toward yourself before digging into the "ass and elbows" work of decluttering.

The first few chapters of this book focus very little on actual decluttering. Use these first chapters to get to know yourself. Face hard things here, first on paper while altering then anchoring your beliefs. Crystalize the ways your life will be different as a result of clearing out your excess stuff.

There is an important gap between thinking about change and actually changing. Begin to imagine handling messes differently. Notice how others handle messes that are different from you. Consider unboxing your shredder. Contemplate a three-bin sorting system in the laundry room. I had this experience when I quit smoking. After trying unsuccessfully to quit multiple times, I heard of a medication that allowed a smoker (me) to keep smoking for weeks through treatment. I thought that was just grand because I actually enjoyed smoking.

Those pills changed my appreciation for the little devils within three days. I licked the proverbial ashtray, quit smoking, and never once looked back.

Compassionate decluttering works by slowly shifting your internal belief system first from "Yeah, maybe I can tackle this mess," to one day decisively knowing you will *never* go back to Madness Avenue again. It will make you firm in spirit that the actual decluttering is done with ease and joy. These next chapters are your nonsmoking drug. Live in your current situation. Feel the groundswell of shifting beliefs as changes to your life take hold inside. Explore with a willing heart.

Compassion and Others

The reality is, some of your old belongings have to leave the building. They have to go somewhere—and *not* in a storage facility. Reprioritize living your values, and your grip on these physical things will loosen. The prospect of letting once-loved items go will become more possible, more plausible. Decluttering with this new mindset expands your newfound self-compassion to others. You will become zestfully aware there are people out there who may need the things you don't and are eager to find them. Getting rid of this stuff alleviates their needs. Donation is an easy way to eliminate excess, which we'll talk more about in chapter five.

Time spent in this working journal will move you through your piles of excess and beyond the finish line to your dream home. We'll work together to expand your conscious awareness and self-loving kindness while developing a fearless personalized decluttering process driven by what really matters to you. Bit by bit, your capacity for compassion, and all the elements that encompass it, will grow. I promise, this work *will* create movement and improvement in eliminating excess forever.

Help

What I can't promise you, however, is to uncover how you got into this mess. What motivated your accumulation or lack of order and how long it took to amass this stuff isn't the focus here. Spending time reflecting on your collections, your buying habits, and your needs and desires may certainly help ease some hearts and minds. Muse on the past if you need to, but do it in tandem with this work. All of this examination of the past is complicated and involves a lot of time. What I know is your beliefs and behaviors must change to positively impact the future. Decluttering demands consistent improved decision-making. Proactive planning. Loving your life more than your things. Instead of looking back, let's make your future more compelling than your past.

Additional support from a therapist, counselor, friend, recovery group, or grief group can help you process past events, which have contributed to your current state of domestic chaos. Use and find the wisdom of a self-help group if needed. Admitting powerlessness over your clutter and acknowledging you need help is a beautiful and often necessary first step in the decluttering process.

Self-care is paramount. I didn't know it then, but during my third year of college, I was depressed, lost, and stressed. On some level, a wisdom's whisper, I knew I was in deep emotional pain and needed it to be alleviated. On a dreary fall day, I made my way to the campus mental health center. To this day I can feel my emptiness. I was in a relationship that wasn't fulfilling, and I felt alone and stuck. My university offered a few counseling sessions that rendered me stable, but I knew I needed and wanted more.

I found Barbara, a petite Jewish lesbian with salt-and-pepper curly hair. Barbara was my guiding light for several years. I loved therapy. I needed tools to make sense out of my role in my family. Growing up, we didn't talk about our feelings. We laughed, we got angry, and we rarely explored any emotions in between. Therapy helped me discover the rainbow of feelings.

Over several years, Barbara and I put my soul back together. With every session, my personal fog lifted. Barbara's questions beamed a light of clarity into my life. Her caring curiosity helped me connect with my inner self, my unique truth. Through comfort and conversation, we accessed my wisdom, and worked to understand my reactions, relationships, and dependencies. Books. Workshops. Looking into my eyes in many mirror exercises. Screaming and punching pillows. My emotional vocabulary and self-love grew. My soul was and always feels buoyed as a result of therapy. Rarely do I feel that fall day feeling any more, though I do revisit my emotional well-being with caring curiosity when dissonant feelings surface.

Some form of compassionate companionship may be helpful for you. You are smart and capable, and will find help, whether it's a therapist, a friend, or in the form of a powerhouse organizer. Partnering with someone in your life who is a great organizer or can serve as an accountability partner to help with the mess *and* doing the internal work may be a beautiful marriage. Whomever you choose to be on your team and keep you on track should be someone you can feel comfortable asking for what you need. Get references. Interview. Make sure you are being heard. Share your vision, then grasp the reins of personal responsibility for this mess in the best way you know, and most importantly enjoy the transformation.

The key to a successful partnership is: When the organizer leaves, will you be able to sustain deep and lasting change? When newness comes in, how will you set limits? Learn from others, but use the project management skills you learned. Don't underestimate your ability to be a teacher too. Ultimately, at some point in life you will need to lead the organizing effort, get more and more efficient, and stop ignoring projects. You can do this. Beautiful stuff, baby!

Fun

Creating a loved home is hard work, yes, but also a rewarding adventure. Give yourself complete permission to color outside the lines, try new things, and find inspiration everywhere. Release the creative and clever person you are. Your inner kid misses you. Take some chances.

Here are some potentially fun ideas:

- Paint-palm handprints framed on a wall
- Loved instruments hung on the wall
- Hot glue fabric or rope to a planter, dish, or basket
- Fun frame collages
- Paint furniture, lamps, or frames
- New homes for old pillows, shells, stuffed animals
- Make button art napkin rings
- Rotate and display collections of clocks, rolling pins, vases, cameras, trip photos
- Attach a whiteboard or a roll of paper on the wall

Stretch your imagination. If you don't make it entertaining, who will?

Not so crafty? There are still so many ways to include fun. The pandemic had a lot of us puzzling and playing games, and of course finding inspiration on

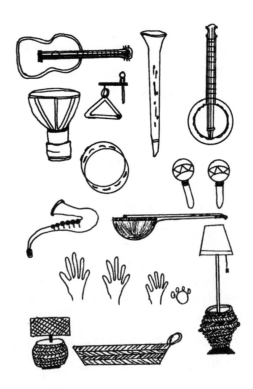

TV. We walked in new parks, reorganized plants, or started the garden we've always wanted. Designing your own "Yes!" day can be big fun.

My northwestern Minnesotan, Scandinavian farmer family worked their tails off planting, weeding, harvesting, baking, building, and doing a hundred other things. When the work was done, it was, "Bring on the fun!" Music, dancing, stories, and general silliness broke out at any turn.

Fun after hard work increases tolerance for doing hard things. Making fun is essential to nurture self-compassion. The blood pressure lowers. Smiles happen more. Some of this fun-making might be new territory. That's OK. I hope you feel this is a safe place to practice self-compassion. Start your exploration through two accountability activities below.

Accountability Activities

The "Soul Survival Pack" activity provides a space to create your self-care plan to comfort your soul.

The "Comfort through Discomfort" activity sensitizes you to articulate your feelings about clutter, ultimately expanding tolerance for discomfort.

The skills you will learn in these activities are:
- Self-expression
- What comforts you
- Self-knowledge of both comfort and discomfort

Activity #1: Create a Soul Survival Pack

Recall moments in your life, from childhood to today, when your soul felt safe, loved, and revitalized. As a young kid, I loved coloring, listening to records close to my speakers while lying on my bedroom floor, and the freedom that came from riding my bike. In the more recent past, one of my most peaceful memories is lying on the cozy sofa in my four-season porch on a snowy day, under a puffy, cottony comforter while watching a documentary. Today, I cook, commune with nature, and practice yoga. What memories and activities revive your soul?

WHAT: Create a survival pack as a self-care plan for your soul. "When this old world starts getting you down . . ." as the song goes, how do you nourish and heal your soul?

WHY: So you have tools in place to rebalance, reconnect, and recharge yourself when doing hard things.

HOW: Brainstorm and record actions or activities that recharge you. Use the template on the next page or create your own format. Access these ideas when the world is getting you down.

TOOLS: One sheet of paper and a writing utensil, computer or tablet.

TASK: Create a "Soul Survival Pack." List ways you rebalance, reconnect, and recharge yourself. List ways you feel loved, safe, and warm.

TIME: Fifteen minutes initially. Add to this list as inspirations surface.

SOUL SURVIVAL PACK

Reflection Activity

WHAT: Notice themes running through your list. Familiar values? Simplicity? Quiet? Action?

: In the space below, answer the reflection questions.

_____

_____

_____

_____

_____

_____

_____

Activity #2: *Comfort through Discomfort*

WHAT: Confront four unique messes in your space over four days. Record your emotions each day. Notice your physical and emotional responses after each daily visit.

WHY: Confronting your messes—your demons and fears—diminishes their power.

HOW: Locate four personal, small decluttering messes that scare, overwhelm, or bewilder you. Stuff stashed under your bed, in a closet, the trunk of your car, or a storage container might be ripe messes for the picking.

TOOLS: One sheet of paper and a writing utensil, computer or tablet.

TASK: Re-create the below chart on paper four times. Visit four messes each day for four days. Record emotions and physical reactions in a log each day.

TIME: Ten minutes each day for four days.

	Location	Emotions	Physical Reactions
Day 1			
Day 2			
Day 3			
Day 4			

Reflection Activity

WHAT: What change in intensity, reaction, and duration of emotion in your body did you experience from day one to day four?

: In the space below, answer the reflection question.

_____

_____

_____

_____

_____

_____

_____

"There is freedom waiting for you,
On the breezes of the sky,
And you ask, 'What if I fall?'
Oh but my darling,
What if you fly!"
ERIN HANSON

Take the leap and soar.

♩

"Up on the Roof"
The Drifters

2 | Attachment

"Nothing is so important you can't be happy without it."
MARTY RUBIN

The hummingbird is amazing. It weighs about as much as a penny. Its wings flap up to an unfathomable two hundred times per second. This mighty yet miniature bird navigates up, down, left, and right at speeds of up to thirty-five miles per hour. A hummingbird dances this beautiful ballet with laser-like focus, constantly engaged in her environment. Why? Because her life depends on her ability to identify that which fuels her.

This chapter's objective is to speak truth to some of the ways we are attached to our possessions. Lead with shameless curiosity. Why do I have these things? Why do I have forty-nine candles when I only light them for birthdays or at Hanukkah? I have closets and closets of bed linens, yet I rotate two sets. Six pairs of garden gloves when one good leather pair is preferred. We are attached, invisibly tethered to all this stuff either in a positive, negative, or net neutral manner. Challenge yourself to put words to your attachment. There's no better time than now.

Focus, like the hummingbird, on the most life-sustaining flowers. Detach from items that obstruct the beautiful ballet of your one juicy life. Identifying ways you are attached to things emboldens you to decide if the attachment is getting you closer to or further from your dream home.

Food has the power to nourish, comfort, and damage our bodies depending on the choices we make. Opting for fatty, salty, and sugary foods is temporarily satisfying, but if we do it excessively and habitually, our beautiful bodies will suffer. Surrounding ourselves with life-giving possessions is as beneficial as consistently consuming healthier foods. In both cases, we are more likely to live vibrantly with greater ease.

Once excess leaves the building, you will notice profound relief. Everyone I know who has gotten rid of excess experiences this lightness and euphoric elation. One of the most consistent exclamations I hear is, "Why did I wait so long to get rid of this stuff?"

Along with good nutrition, the prescription for a healthier life is to identify pieces in your collection that offer feelings of joy and functionality. These treasures feed your soul or, as my health coach Mary would say, are nutrient rich. These *things* are the secret sauce that create a home. Let's dig in and objectively confront your object attachments.

Object Attachment

You are not alone. People everywhere, especially Americans, have an obsession with things. Food, housing, clothing, and medicine are essentials, and I'm not questioning these needed items. The nonessentials, the things we *want* but don't *need,* include electronics, knickknacks, jewelry, recreational vehicles, and excess essentials. In the first quarter of 2020, US consumers spent $14.5 *trillion* dollars on stuff, according to Investopedia.com. Each and every one of us contribute to that crazy number of things we *don't* need to survive.

Everything within our milieu from the cars down to the paperclips are like marbles in a jar, and you are at the epicenter of that vessel. Every item you own is connected to you in some way.

Each "marble" gets a decent place to live, on prominent shelves, under our beds, as a part of our current wardrobe, or parked in protective garages. We appreciate these things at first because they elicit feelings of satisfaction. But eventually, we tire of them, they break, or—most often—something shinier takes its place. So excited, we push the old marbles away and bring in new ones to replace them. Yes, some marbles are given away, but many remain a

part of our lives in some way attached by history and memories. Sometimes we buy a bigger jar, but most of the time, we put these outdated marbles into boxes, out of the way into the furthest reaches of our jar, or even into costly temperature-controlled marble storage environments.

Americans love the storage industry. According to IBISWorld research firm, the self-storage revenue increased to $38.6 billion in 2019. A lot of this space is used for transitioning after death, divorce, disasters, or displacement. Be aware that you are storing a lot of things you'll never use or see again.

I transitioned from a three-bedroom home to a shared two-bedroom condo. Combining two lives worth of stuff, and knowing we were going to buy a house "one day," we stored excess in a ten-by-ten-foot temperature-controlled storage facility for what turned out to be three years. We moved into the new home, and in reality, we only used 30 percent of the stuff we stored. Stuff didn't fit, was the wrong style, or our style preferences had shifted. At $100 per month over three years, that's $3,600. What a waste of money! Lesson learned.

If you've already got a storage unit collecting dust somewhere, take action now. Open the door.

How is this locked up stuff feeding you or adding positivity to your life? Better yet, treat this unit as a confessional. Accept responsibility with pure unencumbered guilt or shame. Decide to incorporate only the most sacred pieces into your current home. Dig in and donate the rest.

Think of each item as an individual person. Every person is in our lives for different reasons, providing us with different benefits. A healthy relationship with things, just like with people, needs your time and physical and emotional energy. With ruthless honesty, acknowledge the *things* in your environment that aren't propping you up. Some are just energy and space suckers, or objects you pass by each day but barely notice. Fillers. Your life needs sustenance, like the hummingbird needs its fuel. With the piercing focus of a hummingbird, seek the items that are feeding you, bringing you joy, purpose, and happiness. Get rid of things that suck the life out of you.

Treat this entire decluttering process as a health and wellness check-up, and acknowledge what you have that doesn't serve you. In essence, you are looking for toxins in your environment. With total honesty, dissect the root cause of your attachment to things. Let go of items that were once loved but aren't any longer. Unabashedly call out those items you keep out of habit and obligation. Without shame, release those purchase blunders. What you are doing is ultimately unearthing those remaining objects that improve the quality of your life.

Love

Treasures under this category were probably received as gifts or heirlooms, were bought to remember trips taken or people we love(d), or are gems that nail a need or function. Items we love elicit smiles from memories and produce little joy bubbles every time we see them. Loved possessions are the keepers. Other things have come and gone, but this item is a one true love.

Here is the tricky part: the moment we acquired an item may have been what you loved about it. Do you love the item only because you love the giver? It's OK to let go of the item and still love that person and that moment.

Items often hold memories of loved experiences. Knickknacks, clothing, art, bottles of sand, and seashells are often attached to enchanted trips, or family or friend moments. Your mind and heart have attached a memory to an item. Objectively ask yourself, "Do I *love* this thing?" If the answer is even a slight no, here's what you can do to hold the memory. Take a photo with you and the item, or record a video with this item, reliving every detail of what it represents to you. Share these captured moments with loved ones. It's OK to let go of the item. I promise you—the memory will always be there because by sharing, you have caused a ripple effect and expanded the memory through relationship building.

In my early twenties, I would shop the Oval Room rack in my local Macy's department store for high-end stuff at clearance prices. I loved the feel of silks, fine wool, and stiff cotton, and even though I could barely afford anything, on occasion I would find a scrappy deal. I will never forget the white and orange pin-striped, stiff cotton pantsuit (oh, the 1990s!) I got for a steal! I loved that thing. The fabric looked so polished. I bought it because I thought I looked polished too. Now I know I didn't want to admit that it never really fit my five-foot frame. I only wore it dancing once, but I had an unforgettable night. The evening with friends will never be forgotten. The pantsuit is gone. The scrappy deal takeaway was that I learned I love good fabric and can't settle for the wrong fit just because it's a deal.

Are you a lover of the scrappy deal? What have you learned from your trail of failed scrappy deals? What were you really chasing? Be honest with yourself, bargain shoppers! Does a deal make you feel smart or thrifty? Then what? Does it lay around unused because you think you might use it someday or can give it to someone, sometime for some occasion? It's not a deal if it's not truly loved, needed, or used. Have a plan and deliver on that plan for all your purchases, or don't buy it.

Pay attention to items that bring gobs of good feelings *and* serve a purpose. Let go of items that don't make the "love-cut." Love will be a tool used in decision-making in chapter six.

Habit

Habit items have always been there, taking up space and doing what they do. They fill spaces, add color, or once served a purpose. These things ended up there and stayed there. Vases on bookcases alongside books we once read. Pictures rarely noticed on walls. Stuff piled on countertops. Lamps in closets. Chairs stacked in garages. Storage bins in basements. To-dos that never get done. Address your habits that have become part of your excess first by noticing.

Pay attention to what you typically don't pay attention to. A few years ago, I was given a fun vase with dried lavender sprigs. Recently, I had just been to a lavender farm in Oregon and was reminded how much I love the smell of lavender. I came home and removed the flower heads, put them in a container on my desk, kept the vase, and donated another vase that was less interesting. Combine moments of noticing with action, and little by little your environment will change. Intentionally.

Habit as an obsession or compulsion is not discussed in this book. Habit in the form of a tradition, routine, or pattern that is hard to give up or change is tackled here. Notice a habit so you can change a habit.

I habitually kept my skinny clothes. Weight gain happens (as it always seems to), and even when I lost the weight and some of these skinny clothes were ideal for me again, I didn't want those things anymore. Too much time passed with my weight fluctuations. Today, I have changed my habit and now I donate.

The same can be true with saving sets of dishes or the "good" towels. You think you'll use the teal dishes in the summer, but you never do. Good towels stashed in the back of the closet are forgotten. Please, use the good towels! Never grab that quirky raincoat? Let it go. Reach for the same coffee cup? Get rid of the others. Does what you think you will do actually happen? Do your intentions match your actions? Pay attention for one day, and identify your habits. Be honest with yourself on habitual behaviors.

During the pandemic when everything came to a screeching halt, I found value in (and the privilege of, I recognize) *not* doing a lot of things the same way. Because I like newness and adventure, each holiday, season, weekend, and day of old was reshaped. I discovered a whole new understanding of what was truly important. During the pandemic, what elements of your past conventions did you find most needed? It may be painful to recall for many, but all we could do was share fun and faces on Zoom. Most wanted and needed more connection. But even now, as the vaccine has allowed us closer contact, something has changed. The need to *do, go,* and *be* isn't as frenetic. Create more time and appreciation for life's simplicity. What are you no longer doing and what excess can leave the building as a result? Don't be afraid to challenge what has always been in favor of what is truly real for you now.

Obligation
This one can be meaty (sorry vegan and veg friends, but you can't say "beety" and get the same response). Things we possess out of obligation are tricky.

I'm sure you know exactly what I'm talking about. The heirlooms. Maybe Great-Grandpa's handmade chest of drawers sits in your garage. If you were honest, you might even say you don't like it or it's not that well-made. Nonetheless, the obligation to hang on to that legacy can be oppressive. Or maybe you received an antique porcelain "Hen on Nest" collection from your mother-in-law.

Having celebrated with her after she found each colorful hen, she willed you the entire flock. She interpreted your joy for her successful hunt as love for the hens, but those chickees will never see the light of day in your modern-style home. Take a photo of the hens. Find a consignor or collector who would love the brood. Place the photo of the collection lovingly next to your beloved mother-in-law's photo. Her passion in this photo will bring her to life more often in conversation than a hen in the closet.

Another major form of obligation comes in the form of gifts. The gifts. The gifts. The gifts. We love our givers but don't always love the gifts. Observe the wine rack, or some other gifted item someone bought for you. Your gut response may be, "I can't let that go. They will notice it is gone and be sad." But obligation is not love. Someone else is waiting to love that rack. Let your friend know it is still loved. You don't have to mention who is loving their gift.

You have permission to let go of *any* gift given. The experience of receiving the gift and its sentiment is a loving moment. Savor that moment. Ownership and power have shifted to your hands. What you do with the gift next, because now it's yours, is up to you.

I have been the recipient of a lot of very thoughtful gifts, even when I request no gifts be given. I am so moved by the effort, time, and money spent for little, old me. That feeling of being loved is the real gift. I hold that most dear. What I do with that gift next is up to me.

Needing to keep gifts because it's too uncomfortable to explain a missing gift to the gift-giver can make getting rid of anything nearly impossible. Here are some optional ways to graciously handle gifting:

- Preempt gift-giving at an event like an open house or birthday party by proactively asking that no gifts be given. Graciously express the presence of your guests as the gift and include your desire to reduce excess in your home. State clearly that you want to leave the event with memories only.

- Proactively preempt gift-giving for all work relationships. When gifts are given for work, confidently state your company's gift policy. State this on every communication as a PS or part of your salutation.

- Place a note on your personal email salutation and all invitations, graciously declaring your wish to eliminate gifting.

- When you receive unannounced, excessive, and expensive gifts, graciously acknowledge the gift and respond with a refusal, stating clear reasons (you don't feel the same, can't accept due to cost, etc.) without drama.

- Gifts received with or without discomfort are now yours to do with what you want. Make sure to include a note of appreciation at the end of each of these transactions. Detangle yourself from obligation. Giver, don't be attached to the receiver's reaction. Receiver, don't be attached to the giver's expectations.

Obligation makes us feel like we *should* keep things we don't want. These "shoulds" slither in like a venomous snake, creating this barrier to letting go of stuff. But "should" and "shouldn't" don't lead with love or need. Personally, I have a fear of snakes and a similar visceral reaction to "should." For you, find another animal you don't want nearby. This is the reaction "should" *should* elicit.

Stop "shoulding" yourself. Family heirlooms, gifts, "might need it someday" stuff, cost paid for an item, and length of time in your possession (e.g., "had it so long" or "just got it") aren't reasons for keeping things you don't want or need.

Should is like a hook. No, actually, it's more like those big yellow tire locks used to secure your car, RV, or trailer. Can you feel the weight of that around your waist? How many of those do you want to have clamped on you? Know you always have options with every should. Your creativity holds the key to the should clamps. Find a friend who might love it, donate it, regift it, put it in a school garage sale, or turn it into something you could actually use.

Purchase Blunders

Purchase blunders are those items you bought with good intentions but that fail to deliver on expectations. The special-order upholstered chair arrives home and is *way* too big for the space. It's damn hard to admit a mistake. All the investment of time looking, money spent, hassle to return, or restocking fees often lead to the big dog staying. Every day you look at the chair with a barrage of negative feelings.

Vacation souvenirs seem like a great idea. They capture an incredible experience. Lock eyes with the (fill in the blank) five-pound pewter buffalo statue on your mantel, bought three years ago, and smile thinking about the Badlands vacation, with the passionate tour guide and crazy roadside souvenir stand. Trust me, a photo with your big smiling face and the buffalo would be enough forever. Next time, take the photo of the item while you are there. The memory is in the moment, not in the item.

Tread lightly through themed festivals and art shows. Yep, you've got stuff from there too, I bet. Scarves and T-shirts. Flowing hand-painted dresses. Raccoon hats. Pottery and sculptures. Wall and lawn art. Knickknacks by the dozen. As a rule of thumb, I walk away from anything I am infatuated by. I am carried up in the moment. If I am still convinced this is a need or want at the end of the day or week, I will go back. Once I'm in front of it again, how do I feel? Imagine handing over the cash and knowing that most of this stuff never looks as good once it's in our homes. When faced with your existing crafty blunders, love the sentiment and let go of any attachment to the blunder. Next time, take a photo *at* the fair instead of bringing it home.

The baskets, bins, bookshelves, tables, storage ottomans, and chests of drawers we bought, expecting them to be solutions to disorder, rendered only disappointment. These "solutions" are often not quite right. They're the wrong size, color, or shape, or maybe they simply failed to solve the problem. If keeping these half solutions elicits irritation, it's time for them to leave the building. Don't settle. Actively visualize the ideal remedy and keep the measurements with you. Earnestly hunt down the panacea, and equally trust it will appear. A patient partnership with the universe will manifest the perfect solution.

Possibility of Need

Holding onto things for years because you *might* need it one day is a lie and the biggest life-suck. Nine times out of ten, you will never use it, you won't be able to find the thing when it's needed, or it won't quite work the way you expected. These "might need it one day" things undermine your creativity. You are inventive and you'll solve for the need when the situation arises. So much goes wrong with the "might need it one day" things that when you finally think you can use them, they always fall short. You end up wasting so much energy, space, and hope on these things, they aren't worth keeping. Trust yourself to solve whatever problem this "need it one day" thing will solve, and get rid of it. End of saga. End of dilemma. Free up this energy to hug your person or phone a friend.

Then there are the things you have but are unsure why you have them or what they were used for. The pieces are obscure. We're unable to remember why we kept them, but since we did, they must be important, right? These random things might include keys, spare parts, or tools, to name a few. I have eliminated and realized the reason I was keeping them, then ultimately didn't end up needing them. I cared so little about accidentally getting rid of these things that I couldn't give you one concrete example. At the end of the day, I don't miss them, and my hunch is you won't either.

The probability that random X and random Y will find themselves is extremely rare.

Keeping stuff that might be important is like watching a car doing donuts all day. A total waste of time and energy. Don't give these random items so much power. You will ingeniously solve the problem today for crap you tossed yesterday. Let go of arbitrary stuff today. You won't miss it.

Enabling Excess

Earnie Larsen was an author, lecturer, pioneer in the field of recovery, and expert on issues such as codependency and addictive lifestyles. He coined a simple phrase that I haven't forgotten from the mid-'80s: "What we permit, we promote." The phrase is apropos to decluttering. The excess you permit, you promote. It's impossible to deceive yourself, pretend, or ignore excess with this mindset. Look at what surrounds you. What excess do you buy, shelve, save, or store? Explore, notice, and accept responsibility for the things we have in excess. Facing the real relationship we have with these things is the ground zero of decluttering.

I'll say it again: "What we permit, we promote."

WHAT DO YOU PERMIT?

Look at your stuff from an objective perspective. Become a casual observer of your environment.

Whatever you pay for, store, and care for—even disregarded things—is a view into what is important. Every habit, like old, unread newspapers stacked in a corner, an unmade bed, a countertop, or a sink full of dishes, has a green-light. Take fifteen minutes to understand what the space and the things in this space reflect about what you permit and promote.

Without judgment, answer the questions below:

What Do You Permit?

What do you permit or say yes to in any given area? Each room or section of a room sheds light on your interests, hobbies, how you manage food and necessities, how you express your creativity, and the treasures you keep.

I am saying yes to: _____

I am saying yes to: _____

I am saying yes to: _____

I am saying yes to: _____

Conversely, look at what you are saying no to. Look for things you haven't dealt with or have given up on. Things you're not fixing. Not unpacking. Not cleaning. What are you actively or passively doing or not doing in this area? Accept what you have given up on. Recognize where you have thrown in the towel.

I am saying no to: _____

I am saying no to: _____

I am saying no to: _____

I am saying no to: _____

Why go through this exercise? Because to actively declutter, we must first identify our habits and alter or eliminate many of them. All judgment aside. Decluttering is a partnership between noticing and changing. Challenge your attachments. Is the reason you are attached to stuff still valid?

What are three things you will do differently as a result of this activity?

You can no longer enable all of this excess if you want less clutter. What we permit today will be different than what we permit post-decluttering. Develop a clutter-free mindset. What will your future self refuse to permit and promote in your dream space?

Growing Resilience

Saying yes or no to things is also about setting limits. Maintaining boundaries is a constant battle. "Yes" to the first donut is scrumptious, but succumbing to the second one puts you in a trance of regret. Clutter is like the donut. More is not better. Damn, "yes" is so much easier. Saying no may be especially difficult for women. Many women have an innate ability to solve, soothe, comfort, and care—and saying no usually means someone will be disappointed. Without regret or shame, learn to put yourself first and say no.

Practice saying no.

- "No, thank you. I have enough."

- "You are too kind. I find I am happier with less."

- "I love your thoughtfulness. I honestly must pass. I am working very hard to declutter and love my home."

Become empowered. Become aware of your truth and then kindly yet firmly act on your genuine truth. This is another opportunity to build self-compassion.

A determined client, whom I'll call Molly, realized after several years of saying yes to housing her parents' treasures, she had tolerated the inconvenience in her home long enough.

Molly loved having family and friends over for card games and festive holiday dinners. But when her parents' basement flooded, she agreed to store the furniture and stored items in her living room. The situation was supposed to be temporary until their basement was repaired, a few months at most, so Molly stopped having friends over until the clutter could be resolved. Unfortunately, her father died, her mother moved into a smaller apartment, and several years later, the flood clutter was still at Molly's house. Over time, she incorporated her parents' stuff into what became a bulging closet already full of forty years of her own family memories and treasures. It was inevitable, as the family historian, that to save this stuff to thoughtfully go through it, she would need a storage facility.

Molly is creative, sentimental, responsible, and tenacious. She had unexpectedly become the keeper of her family's business records. She found safe spots in her home for every paperclip, pencil, knickknack, card sent, and check written that her parents had accumulated. One day she realized she was overwhelmed, overburdened by the responsibility of preserving the family's legacy all at the expense of her home and personal happiness. When we met and I asked about her vision for home, with tears in her eyes she shared her dream. She dearly missed those fun and easy dinners with family and friends all gathered around her big, beautiful table. Molly realized this excess had become a roadblock to the full life she once led. The memories and mementos were keeping her from the people and parties she loved.

Over the next couple years, Molly divided up the treasures among family members, got rid of the piles surrounding her large family dining table, repainted the room, and hung new curtains. In the last year, Molly has had more gatherings at her house than she had in the last decade. And the highlight of her year was her family gathered around her at Thanksgiving.

Molly took control of her situation. She finally said, "Enough is enough! I get to live my life too." She set and met goals. I couldn't tell Molly to get moving. She had to be willing to do it on her own, and she was. Molly made the time, pivoted, and set and achieved her goals on her own with me as her cheerleader.

Cost of Excess

Like Molly, many of us miss the connection with friends and family because our living spaces are cluttered. This is a real crisis. We grow, learn, love, laugh, and live a fuller life when we share time and space with others. It's not the number but rather the quality of people and things in our life. We are better together. I am an introvert. I love (a lot of) time to myself, but I also know I need the infusion of others in my life. As an article on the University of Minnesota website notes:

> According to psychiatrists Jacqueline Olds and Richard Schwartz, social alienation is an inevitable result of contemporary society's preoccupation with materialism and frantic "busy-ness." Their decades of research support the idea that a lack of relationships can cause problems with physical, emotional, and spiritual health. The research is clear and devastating: **isolation is fatal**.

How do you know if your attachment to your possessions is affecting your relationships? Ask. Ask a trusted friend or family member. Know that people love you and want the best for you. Be open to honest feedback. What is it they feel when they are in your space? Give yourself time to process this information without judgment. What part of this feedback could be true? No one can convince you to change. *You* have to come to that conclusion on your own. Often, we are too close to be objective, and a trusted comrade can help create some distance from our stuff.

You are more than your stuff. What this trusted person offers you is a new perspective. In time, you might be able to see value in their input. Fresh possibilities may blossom inside you and shift how you see excess. To change, you need to be open. Believing a loved space is possible will get you closer to clutter-free living. The more you believe a loved space is possible, the more you will see things differently and practice doing things differently. Start with one "No thank you, I have enough" at a time. Each will be a reclamation on the path to your happiness.

Resilience grows as you experience and overcome difficulty. Expanding your capacity to face your truth is essential to move through the decluttering process. Acceptance is an opportunity to grow. With self-care, compassion, and kindness, you begin to honor your truth. You are not a failure. You are a warrior building endurance by accessing self-honesty and your innate creativity to deal with the excess.

Accountability Activities

Daily, like an unconscious dance, you care for and protect these spaces full of stuff. In reality it is a type of relationship, right? So engage in a conversation with these spaces. This first activity is meant to encourage honest dialogue between you and your space. You feed and care for these spaces. On some level, your space is responding. The second activity is a mini-decluttering activity to prepare for a fictitious guest.

The skills you will learn in these activities are:

- A keen awareness of your surroundings.

- Expressing honestly and experiencing empathy.

- How to quickly create a two-person sitting area.

The insights from these activities will be valuable when you are planning and creating the project list in the upcoming project management chapter.

Activity #1: Conversation Activity

WHAT: Have a two-way conversation with your living space.

WHY: Stretch yourself to see not just stuff, but the emotions in this space.

HOW: Role-play a conversation with your space and another conversation your space has with you. Allow subconscious and conscious thoughts and feelings to surface. Mine for thoughts, feelings, desires, dreads, ambitions, beliefs, and wishes each of you are having for the other.

TOOLS: Distraction-free environment. "Safe-Zone Conversation" dialogue starter. Feelings list. One sheet of paper and writing utensil, computer or tablet. Voice recorder.

TASK: Have a monologue with a loved or loathed area of your home. Then role-play the monologue your loved or loathed space would have with you. In the spirit of bolstering tolerance for discomfort, I know this may feel wonky but give it a try. As if this room was human, what are you saying to each other?

TIME: Forty minutes total. Each of the twenty-minute activities should be completed on two different days.

Safe-Zone Conversation Starter

1. You speak to your room.
Slowly, with an open heart and mind, visually scan the area top to bottom and side to side.

- What emotions, phrases, or thoughts come to mind as you observe these possessions?

- Express what you love and where you find joy in this space.

- Focus now on the trouble spots, such as stacks of books, the papers, the yard, or surfaces filled with possessions. What do you want to be different?

- Review the list of emotions below to see if any of them resonate:

Feelings List

Angry	Disappointed	Overwhelmed
Bright	Disinterested	Sad
Chaotic	Frustrated	Unclean
Comforted	Happy	Other?
Confused	Lonely	
Cozy	Neglected	

Once you've finished this conversation, write down your thoughts and feelings about this space on a separate piece of paper. When you're ready to come back to this place, hold the second conversation, in which your space would like the opportunity to speak to you. Embody the essence of your space. Become your space and its contents. Actively listen. What hopes and dreams did this space inspire when you first moved in? What does this space think of you as its caregiver? If this space were a child, how well would it feel cared for?

2. Your room speaks to you.

Everything in this space is able to speak to you. Give these non-living things an opportunity to express themselves.

- What would individual things say to you?

- How does this space feel about the care it receives?

- What does this space want to be different?

- What makes this space happy?

Feelings List

Angry	Disappointed	Overwhelmed
Bright	Disinterested	Sad
Confused	Frustrated	Unclean
Comforted	Happy	Other?
Chaotic	Lonely	
Cozy	Neglected	

When your room has finished speaking to you, write down the thoughts and feelings your space is having about the state of this space.

Reflection Activity

WHAT: On a scale from 0 to 100 percent, how invested were you in these conversations? If you felt less than 80 percent invested, consider revisiting in a day or two.

: In the space below, answer the reflection question.

_____

_____

_____

_____

_____

_____

_____

Activity #2: *Seeing Is Believing*

WHAT: Imagine someone you deeply love and admire (living or passed) will arrive in fifteen minutes. This is the last time you will ever see this person. Create a sitting area for two people, reflective of you, where both of you can sit and enjoy each other. This moment is happening very soon. Don't be attached to perfection. Everyone who enters the room has only visibility to this one sitting area. All else is blurred out.

WHY: Practicing mini vignettes like this helps develop a playful confidence, because seeing provokes believing a functional living space is possible.

HOW: Clear a small area of extraneous clutter and create a relaxing sitting area for two people.

TOOLS: Two chairs.

TASK: Create a clutter-free, three-by-three-foot area and a two-person sitting area.

TIME: Thirty minutes.

Reflection Activity

WHAT: Think about what it felt like to complete the activity. Explain your approach. Express feelings you experienced from clearing, setting up, and sitting in the space.

: In the space below, answer the reflection questions.

_____

_____

_____

_____

_____

_____

"Do the best you can until you know better.
Then when you know better, do better."
MAYA ANGELOU

Honestly confront the many ways we are attached to stuff. Identify your habits, obligations, mistakes, and the shoulds and might-need-one-day items. Then challenge every item. Is it necessary, functional, and loved? Is your stuff fueling your big life or clipping your beautiful wings?

We all have excess. I have excess I confront every day. Just because I help others declutter, organize, and clean doesn't mean I don't need to be careful about my clutter. I work at it daily. Ask my editor. The excess from this book could be another book. Let's all face our attachment to stuff. Ignore nothing. Decide what you love, value, need, and use. Release the rest.

"In Dreams"
Jai-Jagdeesh

3 | Personal Values

*"It's not hard to make decisions
when you know what your values are."*
ROY DISNEY

The goal of this chapter is to unearth and become reacquainted with your personal values. Knowledge of your personal values is critical in decluttering. As you hold your excess alongside your core values, they will help you construct a sieve to assess what makes the cut.

Personal values are a familiar phrase but really an overwhelming and elusive concept. Andrew Carnegie, the Scottish-born immigrant who led the expansion of the steel industry in the late nineteenth century, became the wealthiest man in American history. During the later part of his life, he became a renowned philanthropist. Carnegie expressed the meaning of personal values succinctly when he said, "The older I get, the less I listen to what people say and the more I watch what they do."

What we do, how we spend our time and money, who we spend our time with, and what surrounds us says a lot about what we value. In this chapter, we'll explore and identify your personal values. It's about knowing what makes your unique life fulfilling. Values are the blood, oxygen, and heartbeat of your life. They're the essentials you need that give your life purpose and meaning.

How we show up in the world and what is important to us changes over the years. What made you feel alive at five or fulfilled at twenty isn't the same at forty, seventy, or ninety. Recalling those moments in your life when you were perfectly you captures information about what you value. Values hold the key to what makes you *you*. Let's really get to know ourselves better. Use every "alive" moment then and today to articulate what elements make your life full of meaning now. These aren't your family of origin's values—yes, they certainly inform what you value, but selfishly focus on you to better know, love, and appreciate your uniqueness.

Values are important in decluttering like a homing pigeon who instinctively knows how to get home. Your personal values are a similar internal compass. Leading from the center of your heart, this force of values becomes a true north, encouraging an authentic life which in turn informs your living space. Fortifying a solid connection with your personal values supplants the desire to be blown about by those powerful marketing forces saying, "More is better!"

We live in a very materialistic world. Marketers are nibbling at our psyches all the time. The battering ram of excess detracts from what genuinely matters. What would life and space look like without the external forces or pressures the commercial world presses upon us? You must be in charge of your choices. Imagine divesting from the onslaught of promoters trying to sell you stuff for one day. One week, month, or year. Who are we without all this chatter?

Life's demands and responsibilities are a weight and distraction too. Hunger, thirst, obligations, and deadlines—just to name a few—are imposed upon us all the time, like standing in a paintball field with no fake rocks or trees for protection and middle schoolers taking free aim at you all day long. Those paint-filled pellets splatter without warning, coming from all directions: media, family, friend and work expectations, real and imagined wants and desires. They pummel you until you surrender, and often force you to make rash decisions just to escape the real or imagined pressure and stress.

When we lack full awareness of core values, life can be unfocused and fear-ridden. Sometimes we give the impression of having our feet firmly planted on the ground, being well-balanced, but we're really flailing about like one of those crazy wind-blown characters outside retail establishments. It can be hard to avoid the circular path of the latest, greatest gizmos and trends. Even a dog chasing its tail eventually realizes it's futile and stops the madness. You can too.

Imagine a frightful or anxious king, who guards his castle and holds on to everything. Without discernment, the king muddles his understanding of what is unquestionably important as an enemy army encroaches. When we hoard everything by default, everything becomes important, which results in keeping more than we need. Harnessing our values armors us against oncoming clutter. Stop! Get off the roller coaster! Take control and quiet your mind. Look within this silence to reveal your honest needs and wants.

In his book, *Let Your Life Speak,* Parker Palmer says, "…running beneath the surface of the experience I call my life, there is a deeper and truer life waiting to be acknowledged." This truer life Palmer references is an honest, full, and meaningful life free of external influences.

Extraneous possessions are *literally* getting in your way of creating a life and space you deeply love. Palmer's "deeper and truer life waiting to be acknowledged" is through that mountain of your unnecessary possessions.

Arming yourself with your own values is the shovel that moves meaningless excess. Parting from meaningless excess will lead to your biggest, fullest life imaginable. Yes, clarifying your personal values will make you that powerful.

A soul mired, overwhelmed, depressed, and defeated in front of their mass of stuff feels hopeless, unable to see around that mountain to their beautiful, fun, and exciting life beyond. But personal values give you structure and act as a power pack to clear through the clutter to your one big life!

ONE BIG LIFE

Inconsistency between intrinsic values and how we actually live is inevitable. For example, if being in nature is a top personal value, how many years has it been since you last went for a hike or touched a tree? Maybe you drive by trees on your way to yard sales and flea markets? Acknowledge the disconnect. Skip the divergent sales this week and go bird watching with your birder friend to live a life more aligned with nature.

Living in peace and tranquility might be your requisite value. Yet, late Aunt Sally's red dresser roars at you every time you pass the guest room. Enough! Paint that thing the color of the sky, feel the energy soften, and live more aligned with your bliss. The value of financial security and betting on the horses more often than not clash. If you lose more than you win, a self-help group or financial planner can help shape the value of financial security. Living a spiritually fulfilled life yet being unkind or dismissive of strangers isn't congruent. Volunteer with the homeless and understand how large or small life events led to their current situation. Create congruence between stated and lived values.

Other impediments to leaning into our personal values happen when our true values differ from people we love or are close to. Exerting a different stance can make us feel scared and alone. In my family I was often called the "Black Sheep." Everyone got the memo that the nuclear family came first. My siblings stayed close, found their first love, married, had children, and settled down.

Curious about how others lived their life, I was always challenging the status quo. I was in search of my own truth and adventure. I felt isolated and I isolated myself, always in search of people who valued what I valued. I have had many varied friendships with people who helped me grow and know myself. As you explore your values, the support you find may be in unfamiliar places and faces. We are in this values thing alone, together. What you value is as unique as your fingerprint. I guarantee, your strongest values will reveal themselves once you seek an honest connection with your truest self. Every decluttering project is an opportunity to try new things and encounter and clarify your values.

Imagined values and lived values, like imagined decluttering and real decluttering, are two different animals. Active decluttering is mired in decision-making. Known values help you make quicker and cleaner decisions. The following is a mini decluttering project that can provide insight into *how* you make decisions and what values you hold. Understanding roadblocks to decision-making reveals opportunities to shore up personal values.

The warm-up exercise takes a glimpse into how you make decisions on a small scale. You will declutter one type of item in one small area. The purpose of this exercise is to get a baseline read on your decision-making style (or lack thereof) and mine it for your values. What makes you keep things? What makes you get rid of things? You can't make a mistake. Like I say to my daughter, "You are learning." Let's do this.

Warm-Up Exercise

WHAT: Practice decluttering. This is a baseline values-based decision-making activity.

WHY: Track the maturation and growth of your decision-making aptitude over time.

HOW: Go to a cupboard, closet, or drawer with too many of the same things: coffee cups, kitchen utensils, T-shirts, socks, writing utensils, or other small single-category items. Remove excess items for donation. Analyze donated and kept items.

TOOLS: Paper. Writing utensil. A bin, box, or sturdy bag. Paper to wrap fragile or sharp things. You may also need a sturdy stool to safely see all items if they are up high.

TASK:

o   Pull out all like items

o   Remove items you don't value, love, or need

o   List reasons items were kept and removed

o   Refer to the values listed later in this chapter, and list values in play during this activity

o   Carefully place excess in "donate" bin, box, or sturdy bag

o   Donate excess

TIME: Ten minutes sorting under timer. Fifteen minutes removal and packaging. One hour donation drop off. Total: one hour, twenty-five minutes.

Reflection Activity

WHAT: Which items had a connection to a value? List these values on your paper.

: In the space below, answer the reflection question.

_____

_____

_____

_____

_____

_____

_____

Decisions mired in too much thinking, feeling, or panic tend to kill progress. Values-based decisions are made with a knowing expedience. Discernment is values in action. Not only will this book provide values exploration, but each chapter in this book will help you shore up your decision-making skills so your whole mind, body, and soul can stand confidently in front of excess and make decisions.

Doing more decluttering exercises has another side benefit. Every physical and emotional interaction with excess requiring you to make choices is an opportunity to widen and deepen your capacity to be in uncomfortable situations, growing grit by staying in the decluttering game longer. You're expanding your ability to do hard things, one decision at a time.

Values are crash barriers along the highway of life, making you focus your field of vision. The very successful home furnishings company I worked for used four core values to determine what products they would sell and how they would treat the customer and each other. With laser-like clarity, decisions could be made at every level of the company based on a firm understanding of these four core values. I really latched onto values as a personal guide.

I learned I value freedom, adventure, and family. If and when our family has an opportunity to travel or move, I have made it my life goal for us to travel spontaneously or get the house ready to sell in a week. Every month we have stuff to purge. New stuff in. The old stuff out. Always.

In my house, everything that needs fixing or updating gets done. When the driveway needs replacing, it gets done. Shower tiles aren't sealed properly? I figure out how to do it (thanks YouTubers!) or I get help with repairs. Doing the work now rather than the day we decide to sell allows us the opportunity to enjoy these upgrades. We are ready to roll in a flash. We have been rewarded with our homes selling the first day on the market (for asking or above asking price). My values of freedom, adventure, and family make me feel fulfilled, engaged, and in charge of my life.

I understand and recognize not everyone has the privilege of this ability to react on a dime. More than values, it takes financial flexibility, and often moving means leaving an existing support system in your current community. If that's the case, focus on changes you are able to make within the context of those values. Embrace what is possible through the lens of your precious values.

Triggers

As much as I love the hummingbird's focus, there is a frenetic darting from one sweet thing to the next. They are surrounded by a plethora of floral lusciousness, yet seemingly unquenched. Yes, yes, the little guys are working hard to survive, but excess has an element of what appears to be insatiability. Good deals, garage sales, BOGOs, and clearances are everywhere, every day. Unconscious, forgetful, comfort, and fear buying are packed in here, too. Question frenetic frugality. Like smoking, often it's the rituals surrounding the thing. A comforting rhythm. A reward. All of this is fine in moderation. What is the real craving? Is it getting the deal, the act of buying, or is it having things? Is the reason habit? Thrill? In my decluttering workshops, never has "getting a good deal" shown up as a personal value.

Drill into the value the behavior feeds. Set limits. Pick the best sale, not every one you see. One choice in the clearance rack once a month, not every week. Take back control. You don't have to eliminate the behavior, but modify and manage the cadence of collecting. This is a lifestyle change.

Migrate energy, money, and time once spent chasing stuff to living your values more completely with less. All the while, you'll be growing self-love, loving kindness, and self-compassion through the process of self-management. Now, *that* is a BOGO.

Dreaming of what life will look like when all this mess is gone and taking time to write down the details is a way to call this life toward you. Point to elements you see in the world that you need to live a full life. Buy, fix, paint, sell, trade, or ask for things to grow this life into existence. I have done this for decades, and so much of what was on my list has come to be. This manifestation isn't only available to me. This dream to reality is yours to claim too.

ONLINE AUDIO
The Perfect Day Meditation

Perfection doesn't exist. However, I believe we experience perfection in our lives in tiny moments and memorable experiences over time. Recall a moment or experience in your life that was perfect. This experience may have lasted minutes or months. This is a time when *you felt complete, whole, or right.* Maybe there was complete silence, or maybe divine choirs of angels were singing. Time stood still. Life was more beautiful than ever before. What if we could collect the feelings and experiences and create one perfect day, jam-packed with heart-busting perfection?

On my website, www.HomeCoachHoff.com, you will find Perfect Day Meditation. This meditation allows you to imagine the most magnificent day of your life. Embedded in the "perfect" day meditation are your personal guiding values. Harvesting values from this "perfect" day brings attention to the few, critically important elements that we need to give life meaning. These nuggets are the elements that shape your one big life. After the Perfect Day Meditation and following activity, you will be able to identify your top three values.

The Perfect Day Meditation Activity

WHAT: After listening to the Perfect Day Meditation, you'll be able to describe your perfect day and identify your top three values.

WHY: To harvest your top three values from the meditation to use as a filter when making decluttering decisions.

HOW: Access Perfect Day Meditation audio file and complete corresponding activity to discover your top three personal values.

TOOLS: Computer, tablet, or phone to access the Perfect Day Meditation audio file on www.HomeCoachHoff.com, sample list of values, a notebook, writing utensil, tablet, or computer to write down answers.

TASK:

o   Find a comfortable place to meditate. Eliminate interruptions for at least thirty minutes.

o   Listen to the Perfect Day Meditation audio file on www.HomeCoachHoff. com

o   Complete "Harvest YOUR Values" steps 1–3.

o   Select the top three values.

TIME: Thirty minutes.

Harvest YOUR Values

STEP 1: Circle YOUR values from the list on the following page. Similar values (to you) may be linked, such as Autonomy with Freedom. Feel free to add values not listed below.

Sample List of Values Accomplishment

Accuracy	Commitment	Growth
Achievement	Community	Harmony
Acknowledgment	Completion	Health/Wellness
Adventure	Connectedness	Honesty
Aesthetics	Contribution	Humor
Agency	Creativity	Independence
Aloneness	Directness	Integrity
Altruism	Drama	Intimacy
Authenticity	Elegance	Joy
Autonomy	Empowerment	Lack of pretense
Beauty	Emotional health	Leadership
Being a visionary	Environment	Learning
Bonding	Excellence	Loyalty
Camaraderie	Excitement	Magic
Certainty	Familiarity	Mastery
Clarity	Forwarding the action	Meaning
Collaboration	Fun	Moderation

Nature	Privacy	Service
Nurturing	Productivity	Solitude
Openness	Recognition	Spirituality
Orderliness	Resilience	Success
Ownership	Resolve	Teamwork
Participation	Results	Traction
Partnership	Risk-taking	Tranquility
Peace	Romance	Trust
Performance	Security	Vision
Personal power	Self-expression	Vitality
Power	Sensuality	

Other values:

STEP 2: Circle your top ten values. Without these values life would not hold meaning for you.

STEP 3: Finally, to further clarify your values, write your top three values on the page below. These are those values you would die for. Narrowing them down develops your choice muscle. What top three values do you need to feed your soul?

1. _____

2. _____

3. _____

Use this space to write down one way you can express each value today.

_____

_____

_____

_____

_____

Values exploration is a full circle, life-giving, compassion-filling process.
Values inform discernment.
Discernment is an inner knowing.
A knowing informs clearer decision-making.

Clear decision-making is reflected in everything we value and acquire.

The more you suss out what you value, the more what you spend your money and time on will matter.

Accountability Activities

This first activity will ask you to focus on things you love for one full day. Surrounding yourself with love will intensify the connection to what you love *and* what it feels like to walk in that love all day. This love activity will aid in decision-making during the decluttering process.

The second activity will expose personal values in people you admire. The qualities we admire in others are what we want more of in ourselves. Through admiration, our own personal values are revealed.

The skills you will learn in these activities are:

- The skill of discernment; choose only love.

- Qualities valued in others are values we want to grow in ourselves.

Activity #1: Connect with What We Love

WHAT: Be completely immersed in all things you love for one day.

WHY: Identifying loved items will expedite decision-making during decluttering.

HOW: Be "in love" all day.

TOOLS: Time and freedom to access and enjoy loved things.

TASK: For twenty-four hours, wake at a loved time, wear only loved garments (or none), eat loved food, listen to loved music, make loved movement (or none), commune with loved people, retire in the evening at a loved time and place.

TIME: Twenty-four hours.

Reflection Activity

WHAT: Describe what true love is to you.

In the space below, answer the reflection question.

_____

_____

_____

_____

_____

_____

_____

Activity #2: *Whom Do You Admire?*

WHAT: The people we admire have qualities we aspire to. These people can be dead, alive, close, or distant people you have come in contact with. How someone carries themselves, their ability to remain cool or humorous in tense situations, or their athletic prowess can all be admirable qualities. What do they have that you want?

WHY: These qualities shed light on what we value or want more of in our lives.

HOW: Time to relish in all those you have admiration for.

TOOLS: Paper/writing utensil, computer or tablet. A comfortable space.

TASK:

o   Thinking about people you admire can take place anywhere—in the shower, on a bike, while cooking, on the subway, walking, or in a waiting room.

o   List those individuals you admire, past or present.

o   Below their names, list all the qualities those people possess.

o   Review your list of values for synergies. Refine your values list by adding these ideals.

TIME: One hour.

Reflection Activity

WHAT: You possess these admired qualities. When and how could you express these admired qualities more?

In the space below, answer the reflection questions.

_____

_____

_____

_____

_____

_____

_____

Being grounded in personal values assists in decluttering decision-making. Our living spaces are sacred when we amplify them with things we love and *need*. Gandhi summarizes the trajectory of this full and authentic life:

"Your beliefs become your thoughts,
Your thoughts become your words,
Your words become your actions,
Your actions become your habits,
Your habits become your values,
Your values become your destiny."

MAHATMA GANDHI

Live, such that the inside of our homes matches the inside of our heart and soul. Having a values-driven lens to look through when digging into these piles of clutter encourages easy elimination. Yes, easy. I know, it's a word not usually associated with decluttering. but with guiding values, it is possible.

♩

"Right Here, Right Now"
Cassandra Wilson

4 | Vision

"Your vision will become clear only when you look into your heart. Who looks outside, dreams. Who looks inside awakens."
CARL GUSTAV JUNG

The beauty and work in this chapter is to crystalize your vision of your loved home. A fiercely held vision is the silent but unstoppable workhorse of decluttering, allowing you to move forward with clear marching orders. Your vision is what keeps you patient with needed pauses, to manage through distractions or regroup when overwhelmed. When your vision is crystal clear and compelling, stopping is never an option.

The reality is, the decluttering process can take months and, for some, years. Not for lack of trying, it's just that life throws curveballs. There will be distractions, disappointing stops and starts, intermittent support and exhaustion. Without a vision, the danger is a mind that ping-pongs from idea to idea, should to should, and must to must. It is a game you will never win.

A solidly anchored vision affixed in the heart, mind, and soul will always be there as you move through life's unknowns. Your intentions don't always get your attention. Debra is proof of the value of a solid vision.

Debra and I took thirty minutes together one crisp fall day early in our work together to walk through a vision meditation. Through tears of hope, Debra was able to create a compelling vision *and* was pragmatic enough to know what had to change to realize this powerful image. She knew this would take a couple of years to orchestrate. The home she currently owned was not her dream nor was the office building she owned. Both had to be cleared out, updated, and sold. She checked off weekly and monthly to-do lists and pressed through personal fears. Making design and decluttering decisions was scary and painful, especially because she hadn't made many in years. Yet she gained confidence after realizing the right decision would reveal itself in time. Every part of the process was a practice run for her dream home, which had to be found.

Here is where having an anchored vision is essential. Unfortunately, Debra's mother became ill in the middle of her plan, and Debra became the primary caregiver. Shortly after, her husband needed heart surgery. Debra, a strong, independent, and capable "schlepper" of stuff herself, was badly injured in an accident, which hampered her ability to physically do the decluttering work alone. Asking for help was hard, but we found each other and made a great team. Debra made the necessary decisions and worked through a lot of pain, and I became her moral support, accountability partner, and sidekick schlepper.

Two years turned into five years. She made consistent progress on small and large projects in spite of these setbacks. Debra was always resolute, tenacious, and steadfast. She was compelled by her crystal-clear vision and the belief her dream home was out there. Eventually, the office and home were sold, her husband's heart healed, Debra learned to live with her injury, and she found the new house she envisioned. Because her vision, captured in a thirty-minute meditation, was so solid, it sustained her and remained her focus through five years of detours. Today, with the weight of the journey behind her, Debra finally feels at home and at peace.

Decluttering is never a straight line. Debra the rock star used powerful imaging, steadfast belief, and a *long* list of to-dos. She employed a trifecta of tactics to declutter and redesign an old home, while seeing in her mind's eye a new dreamy space. Her vision never faltered through all these setbacks. The woman's nose was firmly on the grindstone at all times. And now that her vision is complete, she continues to skillfully refine this dream home too. A champion visionary, this Debra!

A vision is a promise you make to yourself. A promise you keep. A promise to deliver upon. Seeing something so clearly crystalizes your goal, and serves as the oil that turns stuck gears. Once the vision flywheel picks up momentum, it works to systematically clear a path through clutter. Literally, your image of your loved home will be translated into a proactive plan in the chapters to come, so it's important to create a clear and vivid image now.

Visioning is like weeding a garden. As a horticulture major, I learned that a weed is anything you no longer want. Unwanted weeds steal nutrients, sunlight, and water. They also often attract unwanted pests. Unwanted weeds are to be removed, and favorable weeds can be moved to another location. Weeds like excess steal energy from your soul and coveted space. Decision-making is like a hoe, scratching out unloved and unnecessary pieces. This. Stays. This. Goes. Hey, maybe something is in the wrong location. Fine. Move it. To personally thrive leave room for only gems that you love. Each whack of the hoe, each decision made gets you closer and closer to your imagined home.

Luckily, this is the fun part of the process because there is no heavy lifting. No decluttering or organizing to do. Visioning is one giant playground, an exciting internal adventure, full of ideas that reflect the "you-ness" of you today. From beginning to end, your vision might change, and that's OK. Switching out an idea with a new idea is a refinement. It's self-knowledge in action.

This isn't a pie-in-the-sky dream. Visioning is the nucleus of a supersonic action plan that you will eventually manifest into your well-deserved, soon-to-be-loved space.

Let's get in the vision mood. To create a more immersive visioning experience, I have outlined multiple ways to conjure your vision. Pick one. Do them all. You decide, but commit to visioning wholeheartedly. The accountability activities will be included throughout this chapter, not at the end of the chapter as they have been, to create a more immersive visioning experience.

ONLINE AUDIO
Elements of Home Vision Meditation

The "Elements of Home" vision meditation activity below is the first drop of oil on your vision flywheel. Like distilling values down to your top three, this meditation activity exposes the top three elements you need to call a place your home. On my website www.HomeCoachHoff.com, you will find the audio activity called "Elements of Home Vision Meditation."

Put on your sensible shoes and take the short walk to the space you now proudly call home. The decluttering work has been completed. The messes and madness are managed. The excess is gone. Seeing your beautiful front door, you feel a spontaneous smile light up your face. Lovingly, you grasp the handle and take your first step inside your sacred space. Welcome home. Describe what you want to see. This is your time to have everything you want, need, and desire for your home. Be as bold, brazen, and wild as you want.

The Elements of Home Vision Meditation Activity

WHAT: After listening to the "Elements of Home Vision Meditation" you will be able to boldly and clearly describe your beautiful and functional clutter-free living space.

WHY: Use your top three elements of home as a filter when you make decluttering decisions to create this loved space.

HOW: Access the Elements of Home Vision Meditation online and complete the corresponding activity.

TOOLS: Computer, tablet, or phone to access Elements of Home Vision Meditation audio file on www.HomeCoachHoff.com. Notebook and writing utensil, tablet, or computer to write down answers.

TASKS:

○   Listen to the Elements of Home Vision Meditation audio file on www.HomeCoachHoff.com.

○   Complete Steps 1–4 in the Elements of Home Vision Meditation Activity to ultimately select your top three Elements of Home.

TIME: Thirty minutes.

STEP 1: Circle the elements of home present in your vision meditation.

Elements of Home

Acreage	Floral	Pet friendly
Adventurous	Fun	Plants
Alive	Glamorous	Privacy/Solitude
Aloneness/Autonomy	Happy	Quiet
Antiques	Honest	Risk-taking
Approachable	Humorous/Playful	Romance/Magic
Artistic	Intimate	Safe
Balanced	Inviting	Secure
Beautiful things	Joyful	Self-expression
Bold	A living legacy	Sensual
Bright	Luxurious	Sleek
Clarity of purpose	Matching	Simple
Clean	Modern	Soft
Coastal	Multipurpose	Spicy
Colorful	Natural elements	Spiritual
Comfortable	Neighbors/Neighborly	Sunny
Cozy	Neutrals	Surprising/Unexpected
Creative	Open	Symmetrical
Cultural elements	Orderly	Textures
Current/On trend	Organized	Tranquil
Eclectic	Outdoor space	Vibrant
Energetic	Panoramic views	Vintage
Entertainment-ready	Partnership	Vitality
Exciting	Patterns	Water elements

Other(s) _____

STEP 2: As in the values activity, practice discernment by honing in on the top three "elements of home" that are so important to you that without them, home would feel lifeless and incomplete. Circle them and write the essential elements of home below:

1. _____

2. _____

3. _____

Don't forget your top three personal values inventory. Write them down here. Together, values and vision are a bigger, more powerful magnifying glass to more easily spot keepers and let go of excess.

Review and write your top three values from chapter three.

1. _____

2. _____

3. _____

How are these two life-giving components of your personal values and your elements of home similar?

_____

STEP 3: Write a mantra using these six words. For example, my values are freedom, adventure, and family. My three elements of home are balanced, private, and tranquil.

My mantra is: In my balanced, private, and tranquil home, I live my fullest life with freedom, adventure, and family. Write your mantra below:

_____

_____

STEP 4: List three items (an accessory, view, wall art, rug, knickknack, book, etc.) you currently have that represent either an element of home or a personal value. Explain why.

For example: The window (thing/view) faces a creek. This view makes me feel tranquil (element of home). The photo (thing) of my family (value) in Norway reminds me of our incredible adventure (value).

1. _____

Why? _____

2. _____

    Why? _____

3. _____

    Why? _____

Vision clarity will expeditiously identify keepers, including items to be rearranged and eliminated. The strength of your vision will loosen your grip on excess. If an item isn't included, it can more easily leave the building. In Chapter 7: Dismantle and Disperse, your vision will take shape and you'll start moving stuff in, around, and out the door, ultimately causing less consternation when the donation truck shows up.

Vision-Making

Vision-making is most rich when engaged multidimensionally. A many-pronged approach maximizes inspiration and allows for investigation from different angles. The process is Montessori inspired. Italy's first female physician, Dr. Maria Montessori, revolutionized education over a century ago. Montessori learning techniques are student-led, self-paced, and guided with free time to explore areas of interest, all done within a nurturing environment.

Similar in theory to a Montessori process, visioning (and frankly this entire working journal) is guided by my ideas, a completely self-directed and personally-paced process. Yes, I shepherd you through each chapter, but what you do and how you do it is totally up to you. Together, we bring enthusiasm, curiosity, and passionate inquiry so you can freely explore your vision here and now. The multisensory "tools" we will use to tease out this vision are:

1. Remembering

2. Visiting

3. Creating

Remembering. Using memory to harvest what constitutes for you a feeling of home. Visiting. Exploring other environments where people live, online or in person. Finally, creating a collage where you gather the culmination of these pools of influence into one amalgamation that is your vision. Unleashing this final creative collage into the universe, along with your belief, will manifest into your wished-for home.

This chapter will make your current vision more vivid or build on a long-held image of your dream space. To envision is to *believe* in the manifestation of your beloved living space to come. Delight in this time of visioning. Allow bold ideas to unfold. If a vision seems believable, be not afraid to imagine the unbelievable. Over time, your vision becomes your super power.

These three mediums—remembering, visiting, and creating—refine the clarity and confidence of your vision. Like those fearless Montessori students, you too will grow in enthusiasm and critical thinking skills as you learn the difference between dreaming and doing. Visioning might be a great opportunity to collaborate or partner with a trusted friend who will help you stay true to and honor your quintessential vision.

"I think that the greatest gift God ever gave man is not the gift of sight but the gift of vision. Sight is a function of the eyes, but vision is a function of the heart."

MYLES MUNROE

Vision – Remembering

I can still hear the creaky, dark stained floors of my Grandma Dagney's white farm home. I close my eyes and can feel the solid wood banister of steep steps that led to her bedroom, where incredible sunshine poured in through two leaded glass windows. No matter what time my sister and I rolled out of the guest bedroom and peeked into her room, her bed was always perfectly made. The consistency, preciousness, and sweet softness of her room was especially comforting. The sun-bleached white chenille bedspread dotted with pink flowers and the lingering scent of her lilac face powder still comes alive in my memory. Bless Grandma Dagney's heart, she wasn't the most accessible grandmother, but she was pragmatic, punctual, and hardworking.

What I loved about this space was the access to nature. We visited mostly in the summers. Looking through her many windows, I saw dozens of oak trees, acres of sugar beets, grasshopper-filled gravel roads, and ditches full of prairie grass. This memory amplified my need for a bright space where I can look out and only see nature, and my desire to have my home feel wholesome, not fussy, orderly, and bright.

Recall moments in your life when you were overcome with feeling blessed, content, and at peace, when a tingling feeling of safety sparked gratitude and warmed the soul almost spiritually. Those experiences are rich with insight into cherished ingredients of a loved life to be incorporated into your sacred home. Crawling into crisp summer sheets warmed by the sun, vacations, visiting relatives or friends, and seeing how other people live inform choices I make today. I like my glassware to match, sharp knives, and a clean counter (for the most part). I take my shoes off when I come home and prefer live plants over artificial.

The activity below encourages a trip down memory lane. Photos of people, places, and fond memories offer extractable feelings. Seek out memories that evoke a feeling of being in the right time and the right place with the right people. These flashpoints are a blueprint of loved elements to be included in your loved environment.

Places that offered comfort during disasters, depression, or times when you felt scared and alone hide elements of comfort. Challenging work projects that became deeply rewarding can provide moments of feeling content, strong, and full of purpose. Hard times can hold surprising essentials needed for security.

Be curious. What made those memories so special? The whole of it. The collection of people. The qualities of the space, the contents, the feel, the smells. When you have an experience in mind, hold the memory. Sink into the luxury of your memories. Nothing is stupid. Every idea is welcome. Enjoy a sense of playful freedom to lead this visioning process.

No matter how small or short a zone or experience lasted, you can find a lot of juicy information to unpack in those moments.

Memory Activity

WHAT: Tap into the past using memories—photos, vacations, childhood, school, relationships, etc.—to cherry-pick aesthetics or feelings you want to include in your vision of home.

WHY: To inspire, articulate, and provide examples of vision to feed your vision storyboard.

HOW: Identify and collect vision-inspiring elements.

TOOLS: Photo albums. Photos on phones or social media. Folder. Writing utensil. Camera/phone. Computer or tablet. Scissors.

TASK: Create and label a "Collage" folder physically or digitally, and collect vision-inspiring images from your memories.

TIME: Two to four hours or as needed.

Reflection Activity

WHAT: Respond to the questions below to inspire and articulate your vision.

List two memories that feel most like home.

What *qualities*, even the slightest subtleties, made this space or time perfect? Comfort? Simplicity? Raucousness? Spontaneity?

In the space below, answer the reflection questions.

_____

_____

_____

_____

_____

_____

> *"Sometimes you will never know the value of a*
> *moment until it becomes a memory."*
>
> ## DR. SEUSS

One wish, even one hope from a memory, is enough to represent your idyllic home. Maybe you have no memory worth building upon. Fear not. Imagine it here. Fantasy has worth and richness. This dare to dream space is limitless. See where the dream takes you. There is value in knowing your wildest dreams because you are getting to know yourself better.

"Home"
Diana Ross

Vision—Visiting

Memory is one access point to conceptualizing your dream home. Memory is fantastic but can be waning or far from dream-worthy. No worries. Construct a vision of what you consider dreamy in real time by physically experiencing different types of homes and spaces. I am a visual and kinesthetic learner. Seeing, feeling, and touching begets believing. Getting out shakes up thinking, activates our senses, and induces immediate reactions. Like those friends that introduce you to new foods or music. Maybe you're reluctant at first but it's eye opening either way. Seeing how others live may firm up what you love and loathe and spark ideas for your own dream home if your own mind and heart are open. We have friends who choose large beanbags in place of sofas. Their active kids love them and life is less stressful for parents.

There are a few avenues to respectfully engage with the living situations of others. Being interested in how people live can be flattering for some, but not all. Make a list of inspiring neighbors, friends, and relatives whose living spaces you've visited. Articulate what you appreciate about them and fully disclose your intention as you ask to visit (physically or virtually). Lead with compliments and curiosity. Share problems you are trying to solve by asking how others appear to have mastered them. Divulging your motivations to make changes and solve problems to create a loved home is always a work in progress. If anything, you will learn you are not alone in continually finding ways to create a loved home.

Walking through furniture stores and tile showrooms demonstrates how beautiful living spaces can look and how problems like yours can be solved. Be inspired to use what you currently have in different ways. Maybe you'll recognize you have similar furniture pieces already. Discover new ways to use pieces of furniture or appreciate the airiness of simplicity. Remove old barriers, rules, or beliefs about color combinations. Recognize when these professionally-designed spaces feel right for you or solve similar problems that exist for you. Take notes or photos (with permission) to capture ideas for your vision.

Antique stores, consignment shops, and art galleries hold promise to be soul-stirring and brew up notions of what you love and want to surround yourself with. Have a walk about and recognize when items spark memories and you feel at home.

Enjoy a virtual home tour. Access real estate company websites. Enter the specifications of your current or desired living space in the search tool available. It's free and so easy. Most homes that go on the market look in tip-top shape, making it easy to scan décor, wall color, furniture, and furniture placement. Notice different floor plans. Usually staged well, they show how people move around in these spaces. Are they similar to yours? How would you make changes? Outdoor photos offer landscaping ideas. Take a screen-shot and save these ideas in your vision folder online.

Pinterest and Houzz have ideas by room, too. Be careful. You can spend hours looking and forget you have a life. Set limits on browsing and have a goal. For example, spend twenty minutes looking for bedroom and office combination or garage organization ideas, cataloging winning ideas on idea boards online.

Capture ideas of home while walking in nature. Make note of what elements of the outdoors are important to include in your ideal space. The sound of water or living plants can bring calm and comfort. (The sound of water can also bring a plumber so be clear about what water represents in this space.) Look within. Are natural elements a part of your vision? If so, look outside. Collect these ideas in your vision folder.

Visiting big cities, small towns, mountain or coastal areas, or other countries and cultures offers fresh influences. Whether you visit physically or virtually, the experience expands what you believe is possible in your dream space. With access to the internet, you can even shop their stores, showrooms, and antique and art shops. Seeing stirs imagination and creates belief.

"Hope & Help" Encourages Inventiveness

When you see your problems being solved by others that means there is hope for your problems too. First, take the time to understand and list your problem areas. What are the problems you need to be solved? Asked another way, when everything is under control, what is the *hope* you have for this space? Take the next step and imagine what would *help* make that hope a reality? Hope is such a beautiful word. Hope lightens the load and gets the universe involved again.

Examples of Hope & Help idea generation are listed below. You'll also find a Hope & Help tool and activity to personalize what hope and help look like in your rooms and areas.

"I hope to put my shoes somewhere out of sight when I come home."
Help looks like:

o   Incorporating a storage bench.

o   Moving an armoire from another room.

o   Attaching closed shoe storage to the wall.

o   Putting all shoes in their rightful closet or location out of the way every time.

o   Limiting the number of shoes in your space.

o   Other _____

"I hope to put my mail in one spot every day and go through mail every few days."
Help looks like:

o   Taping off an area and placing a bin or basket labeled "Mail" in a prominent space.

o   Scheduling "Mail" on your calendar every other day.

o   Rewarding yourself with a Scooby snack each time you deal with the mail.

o   Touching all mail daily. Immediately tossing or shredding junk mail.

o   Other _____

"I hope to have a clutter-free countertop so I can have space to prepare meals."

Help looks like:

o   Removing items from uppermost shelves. Decluttering. Donating or storing excess elsewhere. Then moving everything up to clear off the countertop.

o   Eliminating unused and unnecessary items from countertop.

o   Donating damaged items and duplicates.

o   Designating a "Clutter-Free Zone."

o   Other _____

"I hope to have my family over for a holiday. Everyone can sit in the dining room."

Help looks like:

o   Reducing and moving a craft project off the table to another room.

o   Removing oversized chairs and moving other, smaller chairs to the dining area.

o   Finding free folding chairs online, and donating them for free after the event.

o   Creating a child seating space using mats or blankets.

o   Other _____

Cultivate a problem-solving mindset. The hope is that this activity will help you feel lighter, like things can really change. Believing your problems can be solved is key. Believing is a message of hope sent out into the universe, and the universe is *on it!*

Home design websites are helpful. If you have a problem, just search "solution for [problem]." For example, search, "solution for shoes at front entry." People are so clever and eager to share their solutions to so many crazy problem areas in any home. Don't reinvent the wheel. Choose a couple ideas that would be helpful.

Grab a pad of paper. Start somewhere. Front door? Back door? Closet, cabinet, cupboard? It matters not. Describe your *hope* and idea(s) that would *help* make this space feel right.

HOPE & HELP TOOL		
Room/Area	Hope	Help

Hope & Help Activity

WHAT: Practice using the Hope & Help tool. Identify hopes for your dream space and cultivate help solutions.

WHY: The Hope & Help tool will become a to-do list of priorities to project manage that will help actualize your vision.

HOW: Label three problem areas (closet, shelf, small space, or room). Complete the "Hope" column.

TOOLS: Hope & Help tool. Paper, clipboard or hard writing surface, and writing utensil. Camera/phone. Computer or tablet.

TASK: Research and make arrangements to visit six homes, stores (physically/virtually), or real estate sites with intent to seek "Help" for "Hope." Document probable solutions in the Help column.

TIME: Thirty minutes per Hope & Help issue. Ninety minutes total.

Reflection Activity

WHAT: Where did you find the most help for your hope areas?

In the space below, answer the reflection question.

_____

_____

_____

_____

_____

_____

_____

> *"Everything that is done in the world is done by hope."*
> **MARTIN LUTHER KING JR.**

Have hope. The sun shines after a dark night. Unease eventually offers a reprieve in some form with hope. Don't let go of hope. Never be afraid or ashamed to ask for help.

"Help!"
The Beatles

Vision—Storyboard

When I am redesigning a client's space, after I have understood their problems and hopes I return days later with a storyboard. A storyboard is a vision board, a series of physical images or material selections (wood, tile, paint colors, fabric samples, etc.) that explains how I can deliver on their hopes to give them a functional and loved space. I walk my clients through what the space will look like when stuff is removed, moved, fixed, painted, and/or organized.

As the client's eyes move over the images and materials on the storyboard, slowly heads start nodding. They scan the space. Check back with the storyboard. Often, I hear, "Ohhhhhh, I can see that working," or, "I didn't think about doing that." Hope blossoms in their mind. These images have helped them see how things can be different. The new image replaces the old. Perfection isn't the goal. Rather, we're working to rejigger the old mold from what is and begin to foresee the space in a new way, in terms of what could be, not what has always been.

This storyboard is like a collage, and both are dream-come-true machines. I like to use the term storyboard because you are telling your story to the universe. This story is a powerful vortex of energy, launched into the universe to begin aligning your home and life dream into reality. There are so many stories of people having no direction or hope who, after creating a storyboard, have brought a multitude of their desires to fruition.

I distinctly remember creating a list of qualities I wanted in a relationship, and in 2004, I found that person. The same list contained a number of other things I wanted: a new computer, motorcycle, international travel, to live in France, a home of my own, a new car, and financial comfort, to name a few. I have achieved all of them. Not overnight, but in time opportunities presented themselves when I was ready. You too can see results. I am telling you this list-making is super powerful.

Anchor

A vision is an anchor. It offers protection from being sideswiped by the constant churn of commerce. A life preserver in the ocean of excess. Even when shiny things, sales, or obligations stare at you, begging you (which they will) to come closer, your crystal-clear vision reminds you to turn and walk away.

Your mind's eye will hold this vision, and as you become ready, you will find ways to solve your problems and reshape your place according to your vision. In Chapter 8: Vision Actualized, everything you have decluttered, everything you have learned will be realized according to your vision created in this chapter.

Forge your anchor, your storyboard, using unveilings from prior chapters: self-compassion, relationships, values, admiration, memories, and the Hope & Help activity. Use one of the visual discovery engines online. Once signed up, use the search tool to "pin" inspirational images of any space. Save these images in a virtual board. Label this board by area, make it private, or share it with others. If technology is baffling (as it is for me), ask a trusted twelve-year-old for help. Collect images of furnishings, environments, colors, styles, helpful solutions, lifestyles, and personal, financial, romantic, and whole life goals. Room by room desires for organization and function can be found on these sites and in magazines.

Imagining a space looking different isn't easy, especially if it's always been this way. Consciously or unconsciously gripping onto your old goals and yesteryear's visions comes at a high cost. Consider the physical energy used to clench a fist. Try this now: squeeze your fists as tightly as possible for fifteen seconds. Experience the intensity as your fists tremble. Release the grip. Feel the relief when this trapped energy is unleashed. Letting go of old ideas of home that are keeping you stuck sets in motion new scenarios, new adjectives, new colors, and new ways of creating a genuinely loved home.

The vision storyboard activity below is a way to compel your dream home and life. Tell the universe in any way you see fit everything you dream your home and life to be. Say, "Yes, and . . ." Enjoy the limitless boundaries and just "play house" with complete abandon. Give yourself permission to dream of a space and a life you have always wanted to live in.

Vision Storyboard Activity

WHAT: Construct your vision storyboard.

WHY: Activate the universe in delivering your dream home and life.

HOW: Use any medium (lists, magazine or personal photos and words, online tools, etc.) and construct a visual image of the dream life and home you want.

TOOLS: Large poster board, a cut-up paper grocery bag, or the non-printed side of wrapping paper. A place to house your images (physical folder or Ziploc bag). Computer or tablet to generate digital images, a folder, and a document to create a storyboard. Camera. Scissors. Glue. Markers or colored pencils. Tape.

TASK: Complete your vision storyboard. Use glue or tape to affix images, words, or other decorative elements to display your vision on one cohesive sheet of paper.

TIME: Two to three hours.

Reflection Activity

WHAT: How did you know your storyboard was complete?

: In the space below, answer the reflection question.

Your storyboard may look like this:

"Once you make a decision, the universe conspires to make it happen."
RALPH WALDO EMERSON

Like a monkey swinging from one branch to the next, have some fun. Doubtless your desires will come alive. Your storyboard dreams have now been set free.

"Song of the Soul"
Cris Williamson

5 | Giving Plan

"We make a living by what we get, but we make a life by what we give."
WINSTON CHURCHILL

E ach chapter in this book is also an individual ingredient to enable you to master a clutter-free life and home. You have generated self-compassion, detangled your attachments, and harnessed your core values and vision for your home. You know what you need to live a full life. Things of less importance are now easier to identify. You are in a prime state to construct an exit strategy for excess, also known as a giving plan.

The giving plan has two parts and two purposes. The first part is a tool to assist you in finding local organizations that will take your stuff. Because there are so many local organizations that accept goods, it's helpful to have a place to house their specific information. When you are ready to give something away, this list will serve as a cheat sheet to get stuff moving quickly out the door.

Friends, family, values-based giving, paying to remove, various e-commerce platforms, recycling, upcycling, and lastly tossing away provide other ways to get rid of excess. These options are pretty straightforward, and your temperament plays a big role in which giving options will be a part of your giving plan.

With all these moving parts, you need a tool to stay organized. The second part of the giving plan, the to-go tool, is a project management tool intended to keep you organized, not overwhelmed, as to what is leaving and where it is going.

You are on the precipice of actual decision-making in the remaining chapters. Establishing your giving plan now makes you prepared to eliminate stuff the minute excess is identified. You will thank yourself for doing this work now when eliminating excess begins. Instead of scrambling for giving options, you'll be armed and ready. Let's move forward and gain skills to create your giving framework.

You've filled your cup of self-compassion. With this self-love it's easier to extend compassion for others. Expand your giving mindset. Begin to detach from your excess. After years of standing protectively in front of this stuff, it's time to step aside; mentally and physically let go. Letting go means an imperative transition. "My stuff" becomes someone else's stuff.

With a giving plan in place, you'll feel liberated when you actually get stuff out the door. It may seem unfathomable now, but I promise you'll experience immense joy when someone drives off into the sunset with something that no longer works for you. Other people need (or want) your stuff. They have needs too. Be the engine that helps alleviate and prevent someone else's suffering. The hunger for this feeling is a good kind of addictive.

From Resistance to Resilience

Wouldn't it be wonderful to effortlessly identify stuff that needs to leave and shepherd it out the door? In fact getting stuff out the door is where decluttering stalls. All too often resistance rears its ugly head here. We build roadblocks as resistance that make progress impossible. I will be the first to admit I too can be protective and controlling of some of my stuff. I was raised that there was a right way to do things. I can imagine you may have a similar rulebook.

Being overprotective and governing how stuff "should" leave the building often sounds like this:

- "If I put the three-drawer antique chest on consignment, I need $400 or I won't sell."

- "Cousin Vinney adored that blue flower pot. I should check with him to see if he still wants it."

- "I want to make sure Grandma's table goes to my niece."

- "I am saving these extra towels for my kid's first apartment."

- "When Bill finishes building his cabin, he wants these two chairs."

Waiting for the family reunion next summer, really? Never. This is a stall tactic. Be aware of just some of the manufactured excuses we set up for ourselves. If any of this rings true for you, decluttering will continue to be a slog. These excuses are friction. Like driving a car with the brakes on.

I get it, on one hand this stuff has been wrapped up in *your* hopes and dreams, possibly for years. You've imagined a plan for it. The plan has never happened. This stuff will continue to be in the way of your one beautiful life until you make a new plan and practice resilience. Do the hard work to bust through your roadblocks. You are not a quitter. You can do this!

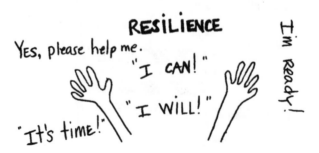

Resilience is the grit you will need to design your giving plan that will get stuff moving. Resilience means doing hard things over and over again. Check in with yourself. What roadblocks do you set up? What rules have you lived with about letting go?

Sometimes we want to wait for the right person or the right time. Bust through this roadblock. Check in with every recipient you think wants or needs your stuff. Is it still true? How *you* feel about an item you give or donate rarely equals what the recipient feels. Your things hold meaning for you, but does the recipient feel the same way? Ask for the truth. Resilience is facing the truth. In reality, most won't tell you the truth. They don't want to hurt your feelings. Most of the time the recipient loves you but simply may not want, need, or love what you are giving. If they indeed want it, let them know the time has come for them to take it. If not, be willing to pivot and get rid of a treasure in a new way.

Ideal Giving Rarely Is Ideal

We often want to find the perfect person, place, or circumstance in which to give stuff away. Maybe the goal was to give treasures to someone you know, who will love and cherish this thing as much as you have. We have promised to protect this inanimate object like a person or pet. Noble but not necessary. The soul of the piece lives in your heart, not in the piece itself.

Gifting an honored heirloom to the "wrong" place or person seems unforgivable. Due to real or self-imposed excuses, we fail to give stuff away because the circumstances aren't quite right. Who loses the most here? EVERYONE! Shrinking to these restrictions, we give up and things never leave. With this mindset the right person or opportunity will never come along. Clutching to this ideal will continue to lock you on a bus that will never move. If this has been your modus operandi then I want to tenderly look into your beautiful eyes, hold your hand, and gently ask, "How have your past plans worked for you?"

Don't be the obstacle that is blocking your progress. Get out of your own way. Let go and experience the results that decluttering magically unleashes. Restrictions and roadblocks are not patience. They are sabotage. Excess control will ensure paralysis. Enough of these shenanigans! Pivot. Get out of its way. Control is a habit that you can break.

I tried unsuccessfully to sell six leather (kind of ratty) dining chairs. Tired of them in my garage, I asked a person working on our house if she wanted the chairs for free. "Sure!"

Yes! I thought. The chairs were gone! I assumed she needed them. When she came back, I learned she had sold them. Yes, I was a bit surprised, yet still ecstatic. I wanted the chairs out of my garage and someone else (once removed) to enjoy them. I got what I wanted, just not in the way I had expected.

Learn to give without strings attached or expectations of outcome. Grandma's dresser may end up painted blue or with a hole cut in the top to be used as a vanity. If you've made it over the bridge to the other side and know you don't want it in your house, then it's time to stop caring about it because it's not yours anymore. Simple. Simple. Simple. Make a decision, act on it, and get it done.

Movement through Mistakes

Even with a great giving plan, mistakes are inevitable. I still remember this large, rectangular, kilim ottoman I sold locally online. The thing was a monster. My partner didn't like it at all! I loved it and thought it was the most exotic thing I ever owned. It didn't match any part of our combined décor, so I relented and sold it (for a dime on the dollar too). Every now and again I feel the pang of sadness from letting that baby go. Then I look around and love what I have in my home today. I see that it still wouldn't work and know someone else is loving it now—or they sold it, trashed it, but who cares? I love my stuff more. You, too, will make mistakes. Believe you will love your new stuff more.

The work you have done to know yourself at a deeper level has made you stronger. So, buck up, little camper, and let's burn these old tapes. Stop fake-planning to declutter, and really declutter!

Forget how decluttering was "supposed" to happen. The plan you had, the recipient, the organization, or cause may never be as perfect as you dreamed. Feel the pull from your new vision as you plan to move old stuff out.

Now that you have a handle on the existence of resistance, roadblocks, and ways to manage memories, it's time to look at *how* to give up excess. People, places, and organizations that share your common values and have compassion are right under your nose and eager to receive your gifts. Let's go find them!

Memory Keepers

Another form of resistance is the memories a lot of your pieces hold. The prospect of these items leaving your space can be scary. Even though things need to go, they have woven themselves into the very fiber of your being. Physically letting go can be difficult because we fear the memory will go away too. Trusting our memory when the item is gone feels scary. I understand the fear, but the item still needs to leave, so find ways to maintain a quick link to those memories without waylaying the decluttering project.

Suggested ways to remember:

- Photograph: Create a memory book or photo folder on your computer. Tell the story of this piece with past and current photos. Ask family or friends to share their photos.

- Video: Tell the story surrounding the special piece. What memories does it hold for you? Like with the photograph option, ask family or friends to share videos of these treasured pieces.

- Letter: Write a little note or letter expressing your love and history of this now-shared treasure. Make a copy and tape it discreetly on the piece. The recipient may find the story special too. Both will keep the story alive.

- Hug: If needed, hold each piece as you express your feelings for it. Make a heartfelt, short, and complete declaration of love and gratitude, then say goodbye. A ritual like this will help you hold the memory and let go of the thing.

- Cleanse Negative Energy: Hey, some things were kept out of obligation or guilt rather than love. Others were just a bad decision that was a waste of time, money, and sacred space. Forgive yourself. Remove negative energy from your space. Safely burn some sage.

Every memory has a life cycle. The better you take care of it, the longer it lives. There is no one way or right way to preserve a memory. Find a way to preserve *your* memory. It doesn't change the fact that things have to go away.

With your compassionate, open heart that trusts the memories will never go away, let's find others who need our stuff.

Greater Humanity

My dad (RIP) was a super sensitive guy. Commercials made him tear up. For me, witnessing acts of kindness, reading, or watching stories of personal triumph and heroism are so touching and heartwarming. Every person has a story that is moving if we are open.

With so much need in our communities, it is easy to feel helpless to address these huge social maladies. Focus on one person at a time. Giving locally can quell so much suffering and provide more comfort than you can even imagine. If each of us reaches out to our neighbor, one person helping another person, repeated by hundreds, then thousands, it would change an exponential number of lives. This colossal surge of compassion heals.

The warm-up activity on the following page will tap into your compassionate heart to support others in your immediate community.

Warm-Up Exercise: Compassion for Others

WHAT: Identify the top three groups of people for whom you feel most compassion.

WHY: To decouple from excess by growing compassion.

HOW: Use the compassion list to identify which three living, breathing, needing, and deserving groups will get your stuff.

TOOLS: Computer or tablet. Phone. Paper. Writing utensil. Compassion list on page 115.

TASK: Write down your top three groups that make you feel most compassionate.

TIME: One hour.

Reflection Activity

WHAT: Of the three groups, for whom do you feel most compassion?

: In the space below, answer the reflection question.

Compassion List

Adults in career or life transitions	Military families. Veterans
Animals	Poverty
Children	Racial and social injustice
Educational outlets: schools, libraries	Refugees in your community
Environment	Religious organizations
Homeless/Housing	Suffering from local natural disaster
Job loss	Victims of abuse
Medical/Disease/Disabilities	Youth

Other_____

Write down the top three groups you feel most compassionate for:

1. _____

2. _____

3. _____

Donation Investigation

Investigate local organizations associated with your top three compassion groups. If you have access to a computer, enter a keyword search (locally) one group at a time. Do the same if using a phone book, or contact your local places of worship for ways to donate your stuff. Contact these organizations to inquire about what they accept, condition requirements, location, and drop-off and pickup hours. If compassion stimulates brain circuits, expect to be flooded with pleasure and good feelings.

The donation list below is a place to take notes on each organization you contact. Use this list or create one of your own. Because life will get interrupted, take notes and pick up right where you left off. Keep the list in one location. Tape it to the back of a door. Use that clipboard you have stashed away.

Activity #1: Create Your Giving Plan— Donation Tool for Organizations

WHAT: Create your Giving Plan Donation Organizations list.

WHY: To determine which local organizations will take your specific excess.

HOW: Research and contact local organizations.

TOOLS: Notebook. Writing utensil. Computer or tablet. Excel spreadsheet. Phone. Re-create donation list.

TASK: Room by room. Item by item. Fill in donation list with your items and exit plan ideas.

TIME: As long as it takes to tackle all excess.

Giving Plan Donation Tool for Organizations			
Local Organizations	Acceptable Items	Drop-Off or Pickup Information	Contact

Reflection Activity

WHAT: What charity most matches your values?

In the space below, answer the reflection question.

_____

_____

_____

_____

_____

_____

_____

Practice letting go of some items with a reputable organization. Experience their pickup or drop-off process. Giving gets easier the more you practice. Remember, even if letting go is hard, the results are positive. Your clutter is gone, space is opening up, and you are gaining strength, grit, and confidence to do more and live more!

Tax Deduction

Donations can reduce your tax burden if you itemize deductions. The IRS's publication on charitable contribution deductions has every tidbit of information on what qualifies as a deduction and lists the fair market value (FMV) deduction of most items.

The phrase "tax exempt" means the organization doesn't have to pay income tax. Exempt means no tax credit for the person donating. Research local qualified charities where donations are tax deductible, then consult their list of qualified items they collect. Choosing an organization that will pick up your items for little or no money would be a bonus. For tax deductibility guidelines, always consult your qualified tax professional.

The beauty of giving to a qualified charity is it can be as simple as loading the car, taking a short drive, and unloading. Poof. It's gone. A write-off. A great bonus and a great feeling. So simple!

Values-Based Giving

Giving in a way that aligns with your personal values is a nuanced way to donate. Releasing possessions to someone or an organization with like values has a multilayered effect. It deepens your connection to your personal values, enriches others' lives, serves as an act of love, and ultimately eliminates your excess. Living life aligned with your values awakens a protected heart and grows compassion for self and others.

Reflect on your top three personal values from chapter three, and write them down here.

1. _____

2. _____

3. _____

Below are some ways to imagine weaving personal values and possessions. For example, if you value service to the community or country, then law enforcement, veterans of war, or military personnel may be your go-to people. There are a number of outlets supporting these heroes that would gladly take your stuff. Seriously. Anytime. I'm talking *this week*. Below are other examples.

Value: Autonomy

Any organization or charity which helps others build skills of self-reliance and independence falls into this category. Groups may focus on trades (construction, plumbing, electrical, etc.), education and job training, or job search organizations. Choose to help those struggling with poverty, domestic abuse, or developmental disabilities live with more independence and dignity.

Brainstorm. What items do you have that would benefit this type of organization?

_____

_____

_____

Value: Adventure or Nature

Explore foundations or charities that help people engage with nature, bring individuals from inner cities to the outdoors, provide camping tools or equipment for outdoor adventures, teach outdoor survival or problem-solving skills, or protect and heal the environment.

Brainstorm. What items do you have that would benefit this type of organization?

Value: Joy, Spirituality, Creativity, Art

Consider donating to organizations that assist others in expressing creativity. Arts and craft supplies, fabrics, yarn, musical instruments, sheet music, or furniture are all valuable contributions to theater groups, cultural groups, or charities with spiritual outreach programs. Donate your collection to local museums or other collectors.

Brainstorm. What items do you have that would benefit this type of organization?

Value: Family, Health, or Social Justice Support

Choose a charity or community organization which helps families stay to-gether or move into an apartment or home, or which repairs homes for residents. The gift of furnishings, linens, cookware, clothing, personal-care products, and school supplies are welcome to those getting started or back on their feet.

Those who suffer from health issues and injustice, and marginalized groups such as LGBTQ, elderly, communities of color, and abused and neglected people or animals all deserve dignity. Your contribution may be the first time they've ever felt or experienced kindness.

Brainstorm. What items do you have that would benefit this type of or-ganization?

Giving Plan—Other To-Go Options

Donating to local organizations including values-based giving are great ave-nues for giving. There are other to-go options. Below I've outlined several other ways to get stuff out the door. The to-go tool can be used to research and flesh out a few ideas that may be a good fit for you. A good fit means low stress, efficient, and effective at getting rid of excess.

Familiarity

Immediate friends, family, neighbors, religious organizations, and community centers may be struggling themselves or may know someone who needs a hand up. If you don't ask, you'll never know. Communication can be done through phone, text, email, and private social media accounts. Spread the word. Let people know what you have to get rid of. Provide photos and dimensions, and disclose any issues to ensure your item gets out the door faster.

Free!

Some items are not acceptable for donation and are of little or no monetary value, but still have use left in them acceptable to many users. People have unique spaces, situations, or problems that need a creative solution.

Many people love to make something out of nothing. Upcycling is the use of discarded objects that are repurposed into something else. A bunch of corks glued together could become a cleverly designed corkboard, or painted cinder blocks could become planters for beautiful flowers. Don't underestimate the needs and creativity of people in your neighborhood.

Look at "misfit clutter" with a new perspective. Furniture that is a bit worn, dining chairs with loose legs or stained seats, and desks with missing drawers or broken glides might be the perfect find for someone who is handy or artistic when it comes to repurposing items. The "free" audience has a "take it like it is" attitude. A truly lovely shame-free zone.

On my local free site, I have listed a dozen old pieces of wood, bookcases with no shelves, wonky metal garage shelving, a rusted basketball hoop (still in the ground!), and moving boxes. Everything was gone in one to two days with very little contact or conversation.

The "keep things out of the landfill" movement is magical and super efficient. Check your local community's online free giving sites. *Give away for free* is a great online search. Find a reputable site. Almost anything, no matter the condition, could find a new home using this tool. Take a photograph and write a brief description with dimensions of the item(s). Determine a legal, neutral location where the item can be found, like a safe spot on or near your property. Schedule a meeting or make it "first come, first served." Let folks know you are or are not monitoring your post. Free stuff creates a very quick "feeding frenzy," and depending on where you live, it is generally over quickly. So satisfying!

Pay to Remove

If removing excess can't be free, then let it be easy. Unfortunately, the other easy way to get stuff out the door is to use a "junk" removal company, which can be expensive. But the good news is, with one call, a truck with strong people will be outside your door to remove every unwanted item, no questions asked. Their fees are usually based on the quantity of space your stuff takes on their truck. Responsible companies will recycle and dispose of items properly to minimize what ends up in our landfills. Please choose wisely. Mother Earth thanks you.

E-Commerce

Often people want to recoup expenses or reach a broader, more niche audience. Many online e-commerce platforms (Craigslist, Nextdoor, Facebook Marketplace, etc.) are available locally.

Anytime you meet strangers for any transaction, safety is paramount. Here are some tips:

- Transact business locally. Get phone numbers. Call the number back to confirm the person is legitimate.

- Use a prepaid phone and separate email for selling items.

- Protect your identity. Keep home address and license plate numbers out of every photograph.

- Never meet at your home. Meet at a well-lit public location.

- Bring someone with you to every interaction or transaction.

- If you must meet at home, have two or more of your people present. Never allow anyone to go to the bathroom or distract you from the sale.

- Always transact in cash. Never take checks or cashier's checks. Consider them to be fraudulent.

- Get the cash first and count it before the item is handed over.

- Be diligent and don't get complacent.

What is the motivation to sell online? Do you feel the item(s) are worth money beyond the benefit of a deduction? Was the initial investment hefty? Would cold hard cash-in-hand soften the blow? Is your item unique and desirable? The more items like yours there are for sale, the longer it will take to sell and the less you'll get for it. Your stuff should sell first if you have the lowest price or it's in the best condition. Having sold many items online, I can tell you price and demand are king. Price it to move.

Selling online is relatively easy *if* the item is in demand. Online sales take a lot of time, skill, patience, dedication, and communication with potential buyers. Vetting scammers is necessary and inevitable. Online sales can slow the decluttering process down with layers of technology and communication, not to mention the no-shows and in-home congestion as exiting stuff waits to find a new home. Time and space are valuable resources. Do you have excess of either? If not, consider another option.

The more information you provide up front, the less back and forth communication is needed. Most important, be truthful to your buyer. Here is a list of logistics for getting a piece ready to sell online.

- Clean every item.

- Research comparable items on multiple online sites.

- Take and attach good photos of each item from several angles and in a well-lit environment.

- Include measurements (height, width, length, diameter, etc.) of each item.

- Add information on condition, including missing parts, damage, nicks, scratches, etc.

- What makes your item unique? Suggest new ways to use your piece. Be enthusiastic.

Post your for-sale ads on a trusted local site. Beware of scam buyers, especially if you are selling high-priced items. Questions will ensue. Update your ad to fill in missing information. Be responsive. Most buyers look at many of the same items or at many *other* items they need or want. Excellent customer service skills are critical. Refresh or repost the ad every couple of days.

Honestly evaluate your tolerance for online sales. What financial payoff would make selling online worth it? If you expect 50 percent of the original cost and get 25 percent, is it worth your time? The current market will determine the value, not what you paid for the item. Lowest price and best quality pieces often sell first. Suggest creative uses for the item. Don't get stuck on the price you paid for something. That money is gone. Extended radio silence will tell you to reduce the price.

Eventually the right person will show up. When you see someone walk away with their new item, and they are so excited, this part of the process can feel very rewarding.

If posting online is not appealing and you want to speed up your giving plan, I suggest posting on FREE sites or surrendering and giving it to your crabby in-law.

Recycling

The Environmental Protection Agency (EPA) has a list of common recyclables (epa.gov). Contact your county's recycling organization or your local waste hauler's website. Every part of the country has specific recycling capabilities and expectations you need to follow.

What you cannot donate, consider recycling. Stacks of old newspapers, magazines, cardboard, glass, certain plastics, and plastic food containers are recyclable. Check out your region's drop-off locations for some larger appliances like dishwashers, dryers, freezers, heat pumps, hot water heaters, microwaves, and some refrigerators. Other household materials like carpet, florescent light bulbs, mattresses, electronics, and even stained or ripped clothing and curtain fabrics may be recyclable. Some items may have a charge associated with recycling them. Many local retailers recycle plastic bags, and local refuse collectors can help you navigate your recycling options. Recycle as much as possible.

Household Chemicals, Electronics, and Construction Materials

Many counties operate recycling centers of household chemicals, electronics, and construction materials. Household, lawn, and garden chemicals, as well as batteries, needles, scrap metal, magazines, glass jars, cardboard, some electronics, and tires, can be dropped off, all with proof of residence. Many items can be dropped off for free. Call or go online for current recycling guidelines.

Many retailers that sell paints, stains, and electronics also act as a drop-off site. Unopened paint stored in a temperature-controlled area can keep for ten (latex/acrylic) to fifteen (oil-based) years. Opened paint needs to be stirred and brushed on newspaper or paper grocery bags. The paint is generally usable if it is smooth with no lumps or debris. Reseal and keep for touch-ups. If it isn't a current color, get rid of it. Take a photo for your records if needed.

New or in good condition construction materials like wood, unopened paint or stain, kitchen cabinets, wall board, nails, grout, sinks, wall lights, appliances, or furniture can be recycled. Local organizations sell these materials, raise revenue, and train disadvantaged people in the construction trade. Habitat for Humanity's ReStore uses their profits to support Habitat for Humanity's mission of preserving and building shelters for families so they can live with dignity in a home.

Toss

Despite only representing 5 percent of the world's population, the US generates more waste than any other country in the world, and in less than fifteen years, worldwide waste is expected to double. As your home coach, I have one ask: may the landfill be your last option. There are so many easy ways to share your stuff with someone nearby. Please be mindful of our one earth. Thank you.

Skills and Temperament

Every giving avenue has pros and cons. Every situation is unique. Assess your temperament, skills, and time. If time is limited, a multi-phased giving plan won't be ideal. Try the family or free community. Are your computer skills limited? Online selling may not be a good fit. On social media? Networking with those in your social network may bring leads. If you want to give stuff based on values, often you have to sell those things first because most organizations want money. Assess *your* temperament and available time to find *your* perfect giving plan.

I would enthusiastically encourage you to use giving options that you are already good at. If you've never touched a computer, don't plan on selling things online as your first option. If you've lost touch with family, don't start tracking them down now. Keep your exit plan simple and expand as you gain confidence and skill.

The ultimate goal is to get rid of excess as simply as possible. Brainstorm below the giving method(s) that appeal to you.

1. _____

2. _____

3. _____

Even contemplating these giving options has stretched your capacity for discomfort. You researched options. Stretched further. Made a plan. Exceptional! Now it's time to create the tool that will help you list items that need to go.

Here is the deal: a lot of the random stuff lying around your house can find a new home. A little investigation, asking around, and giving away are all ways excess will eventually leave. You've done work accumulating. Now you are doing this work in reverse. Easier and faster. You are so close to changing your life forever. Tools and tenacity are key but you can't get there without a plan.

To-Go List

The to-go list is a project management tool, a master plan of all items that are leaving. Start one room at a time. Identify items in each space that will be on the chopping block. Activity #2: Creating a "To-Go" List is an opportunity to think about what and how you might get rid of your items. Bring your vision along for the ride.

Giving Plan To-Go List by Room			
Room	Item	Giving Plan Option	Gone

Activity #2: *Creating a "To-Go" List*

WHAT: Create your own "to-go" list.

WHY: To organize what and how excess leaves.

HOW: Visit each living space. Fill out all columns for each known item that is leaving.

TOOLS: Notebook. Writing utensil. Computer or tablet. Excel spreadsheet. Re-created to-go list.

TASK: Room by room. Drawer by drawer. Shelf by shelf. Write in your to-go list what goes and where it goes.

TIME: As long as it takes to tackle all excess.

Reflection Activity

WHAT: When do you feel powerful and in charge?

In the space below, answer the reflection question.

_____

_____

_____

_____

_____

_____

_____

Below are ways to approach filling in the "item" column on your to-go list.

- If your home has multiple levels, start at the top floor and work your way down, or start at the lowest level and work your way up.

- Work from the least busy space to most busy space.

- Start in the easiest space and work your way to the most challenging or vice versa.

Maybe begin with the "no-brainer" easy stuff that deep down you know has to leave, like a disliked rug, empty plant pots, too-thick or too-thin socks, a three-pronged rake you haven't used in years, and outdated electronics. Whatever you decide, keep the process simple, easy to remember, under-standable, and repeatable.

Be aware of stuff that no longer feeds your values or vision. Subsequent chapters will cause you to make additions and refinements to this list as you become clear how you want to escort stuff out the door. Delete. Cross out. Add. Recycle the old list. Make a clean list. Each pass leads to new awareness. Your giving plan will take shape.

This to-go list is a project manager's road map. A plan to get and stay or-ganized. In subsequent chapters, you'll tackle making final decisions and doing the decluttering. The to-go list *and* your vision are two project management tools that will be present for the duration of your decluttering process. The to-go list is so important because it is *the* decluttering action plan to ulti-mately manifest your vision. Take this list seriously. It is your vision partner.

Lists Not Your Thing?
Not a list maker? Try the color-coded sticker system. Place a colored sticker on a piece that identifies what and where the item is going. For example:

Red=Donate, Green=Family/Friend, Yellow=Sell/Free. If you don't have stickers on hand, you can use tape, too. Don't buy stickers or tape. You probably have some. Make a key for your system. Post it on a wall. Keep your key easy to understand and remember.

Practice

Practice letting go of any no-brainer items. Let's take those empty plant pots. If you have a giving plan, fill it in on the to-go chart. Take the next step and do one thing to get the pots out the door. Call, email, and take and send photos to someone you think might want them. If you have a donation center in mind, check the hours and their list of acceptable donation items.

If you're not there yet, practice donating by placing donation items out of sight: in the trunk of a car, garage, or another safe, out-of-the-house place. Avoid storing them in the basement or another room. Ensure these items physically leave the building to make it more real that they are gone. There are two reasons for this. One, to experience the physicality of moving excess, and two, to luxuriate in some open space where the item(s) once was. You may be having a rainbow of emotions, from sadness, to relief, to maybe a sliver of gratitude. Acknowledge what feelings you are experiencing.

The beautiful thing is breath and blood flow are still happening. Life is still moving forward. You are alive, well, *and* practicing letting go. Yes, for some this is easy. For many this may be painful. For some any progress is truly something to be giddy about. Honor where you are right now.

The good news is, the pain will lessen as you continue to let go. Eventually the items you've temporarily stashed in the garage or trunk will be gone. The act of giving may not be a well-developed skill or habit, but with time tolerance blossoms.

One elephant yet to be discussed that is still in the room is paper. How do we get rid of all this *paper?* I had a whole chapter on paper. I decluttered it and want you to do the same.

Paper

For a digital society, why is there still so much paper to manage? I would say paper is the bigger nemesis for people with and without clutter issues. Paper is something you control. The less you bring in, the less you'll deal with. Regulated and consistent paper management is essential. Forever.

Paper has to be dealt with. Here are a few ways to eliminate excess paper.

Online bill pay may be your jam, but for those that like paper, you have work to do. The excess has to go. Recycle, shred, and give are options.

Shred, then recycle excess paper containing any personal information using a more secure, multi-directional shredder. Research free shredding opportunities online. Local cities, churches, and some counties offer periodic shredding for free or for a small donation. Non-personalized paper can be recycled.

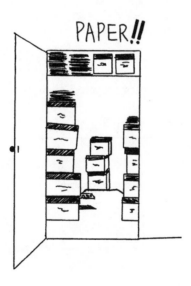

Short-Term Paper

Short-term paper is anything you need access to within the tax year. Here are some ideas of what to keep in a hanging file system with categories like:

- Childcare

- Bank statements

- Bills to be paid

- Bills paid (Use paperclips for each account payable. When they're reconciled, shred them.)

- One outgoing mail spot or folder

- Household repairs, insurance, and improvements

- Insurance policies

- Medical

- Pets

- Current tax documents: medical, taxes, paid bills for itemizing, etc.

- Transportation: cars, motorcycles, snowmobiles, RVs, etc.

- Warranties, receipts, and manuals

Check your home first for hanging file folders with labeling tabs. Find them on a local giving site or at an office supply store if needed. Keep your filing system simple. Personalize the categories that work for you. Paper sitting around for over a year that isn't long-term paper can be tossed or recycled.

Long-Term Paper

Long-term files can be stored out of sight or in a secure, moisture-free environment. These records are rarely accessed but they do need to have a spot.

A lot of long-term paper includes things the government needs for taxes, receipts or proof of purchase or sale of large assets (home/car), legal status documents, warranties, and assembly instructions, to name a few. See a more complete list below:

- Past seven years of tax records (consult accountant for exceptions)

- Legal documents: titles, birth certificates, passports, wills, trusts, marriage certificates, etc.

- Warranty information. Label each manual, warranty expiration date, and assembly instructions.

- Health and medical records

- Receipts for household repairs, insurance claims, and improvements

- Consult an accountant for other documents that may be needed

Label a file box "Long-Term Storage" and list contents. A dry basement, under beds, or in rarely used closets are good choices for long-term paper storage.

Tax Papers

The IRS website lists the specifications for financial records and the receipts required for tax purposes. Publication 552 is helpful for organizing tax paperwork. Below are some of the topics this publication covers.

- Why Keep Records?

- Kinds of Records to Keep

- Basic Records

- Specific Records

- How Long to Keep Records

- How to Get Tax Help

If the government requires certain papers kept, then also accept the fact that papers not on that list do not need preserving. Please note, insurance companies or creditors may require records are kept longer than the IRS, so follow up accordingly.

Other Paper

Consider giving magazines, newspapers, or books on CDs or DVDs to prisons, local thrift stores, donation centers, used book stores, senior living centers, libraries, hospitals, family or women's shelters, and military organizations. Be sure to remove or blacken your address information on all magazines.

Hardcover books, because of the glue and binding, are often hard to recycle, so consider donating them to local theater production companies and home furnishing stores for display purposes. Some of these items can be used for craft projects at preschools, day cares, or local non-profit art organizations.

Time

Do not spend a lot of time on finding *the best* home for every single item. This is what caused your clutter problems in the first place. Establish a timeframe, like two weeks, to find a new home for these things, and if no home is found, donate or give them away. As a last resort, toss them in the trash if acceptable to your hauler. Whatever dream accompanied this stuff has passed. Acknowledge the missed opportunity and sweetly send it out the door. Promise that XYZ will be gone by a reasonable date, and hold yourself accountable to this timeline.

Four ways to hold yourself accountable to a timeline:

1. Daily prompt—"Less is best because_____."
2. Calendar reminders—Set reminders mid-timeline, two days prior, and on the final day.
3. Accountability partner—Confide in a friend about your goal.
4. Reward—When you reach your goal, plan time of unabashed nothingness with a friend. Find free events in your neighborhood, watch a movie, take a walk, or go get a treat. Find familiar fun or try a splash of something new.

The next two chapters are the doing of decluttering. Touching things. Moving things, many of which will end up on your to-go list. Familiarizing yourself with giving options now will ensure great success as the decluttering project really begins. The project manager always has a plan.

"It's not how much we give, but how much love we put into giving."
MOTHER TERESA

Getting rid of excess is *the* reason we are here together. We are refining your unique and precious life, learning to keep only what is loved, used, and needed, and letting the rest serve others. Be generous of heart and home so others feel your love and are forever changed.

♩

"Your Love Is Lifting Me Higher"
Jackie Wilson

6 | Choices

"I believe we are solely responsible for our choices, and
we have to accept the consequences of every deed,
word, and thought throughout our lifetime."
ELISABETH KUBLER-ROSS

E very minute of the day, choices befall us. Should I shower or not, eat cereal or toast, wear the blue or yellow shirt, jeans or slacks, walk or bus? All this within the first thirty minutes of a day. We make thousands of choices each day, and so many are made subconsciously. All choices made often and repeatedly can become exhausting. When we have to think and weigh options, we trigger our emotions and worry about possible consequences. We stop making decisions, or rigidity creeps in and leads to stagnation. Either way, the wheel that powers decision-making stops. For many, this is the very cause of clutter.

Our goal here together is to make malleable those hardened edges of stagnation. You have more skills now. Harness decisiveness. Let's saddle up and get going again. With self-compassion emerging and accountability expanding, you have more grit in the bank. You have resuscitated your personal values and vision to aid in establishing boundaries. Narrowing your framework and considering only loved and needed things is everything you need to keep the wheels of the decision-making bus lubed up and running smoothly.

The intrapersonal work you have done thus far is awe-inspiring, necessary, and foundational. My hope is that you know yourself better, you are less afraid to address your messes, and you may even feel hopeful.

Now let's add more tools to your decluttering toolbox. Learn, relearn how to make choices. I have three simple ways to practice choosing. Bring your whole self *and* choosing skills to the decluttering party which, may I remind you, begins in the next chapter.

This is the time to believe you are capable of successfully making decisions. In her book, *The Art of Choosing,* Sheena Iyengar says, "In order to choose, we must first perceive that control is possible." Do you believe you can manage one mess? Because all you start with is one mess. Confidence in getting things under control *is* the name of the game. Let that notion wash over you.

Have faith in your ability to take command of one little mess. The whole of it is too much to conceive. Take decluttering in one bite-sized bit at a time. Rome wasn't built in a day, and there are many steps in a marathon. Pick up one brick, take one step, deal with one small pile, and decluttering success will be yours!

Choice Tools

We want to know we have made the best choice. Trust yourself. You will make the best choice you can with the information you have, *today.* Don't worry about past or future choices. The following three choice tools will help you make good choices. Making, not avoiding, choices is good parenting. Choices construct and honor boundaries. Have the curiosity of a Montessori kindergartener, and explore different ways to make choices and let go of excess.

The three choice tools are (in no preferential order):

1. Love It or Lose It

2. No Space = No Place

3. Need vs. Want

The next chapter is the dismantle and disperse process. Where the "ass and elbows" work of decluttering begins. Right now, you are mentally and emotionally making choices on what stays and goes. Making choices is the *power center* of decluttering. Two things are happening: you're setting limits and beginning to separate from your excess.

As you review these three choice tools, know you can use one choice tool exclusively, move between all three, or come up with your own. Doing nothing isn't an option if you want real change.

Choice Tool 1: Love It or Lose It

"Love It or Lose It" starts with love. Loved items produce smiles from the inside, making you feel radiant and warm. You love looking at it, wearing it, using it. Love. Love. Love. Think Marie Kondo's amazing decluttering book *The Life-Changing Magic of Tidying Up*. Liking something, or feeling like it's "just OK" is not love. Lead your decision-making with love. Sounds so easy, yet true love you can't live without. True love is fulfilling, is nourishing, and actively adds to your life. You love how useful this thing is and how it makes you feel. Got something negative to say about this thing or only love its memory? Take a photo and send it on its way.

Every item goes through the love test. Lamps, pillows, candles, frames, old and new kitchen gadgets, toys, pottery, baskets, fiesta ware, beer cans, dolls, Victorian furniture, garage and yard goods. The rating scale is simple:

1. Love and keep it.

2. Donate, give, sell, or recycle it.

Having two options is intentional. A third choice complicates and dilutes the process. Your ability to discern what true love is will help you make quick decisions. Sure, you may have to go through a pile a couple times, but each time you do, your resilience and clarity grows.

Your number one items might include clothes that look and feel terrific when you wear them. These items breed compliments like a pheromone that others notice. Number ones produce this allure. Honestly, I got rid of a lot of things that I realized I never loved. I kept them because they "worked," but I didn't feel good in them nor did they elicit compliments. Number ones are your best friend. A handful is all you need.

Quantity is a false profit. Choose a love connection over quantity. Yes, this will seriously limit what is left. You only need a few number ones, because these pieces are pleasing on multiple levels. Hold up each item, wear it, use it, display it. Put the item in question into the mix right now. Honestly ask yourself, "Does this item fit my definition of love?" If you were given this piece today, would you want it? Loving something for the purpose it fulfills works too.

Keeping extraneous things is a habit, and it drowns us in mediocrity. We become afraid there will be so little left we convince ourselves to keep it because "more is better," or we might need it "someday." But by the time "someday" rolls around, we have forgotten or can't find the thing. Feel the weight of that habit pressing down on your shoulders. To keep only number ones is life-giving. Period.

Practice letting go of unsentimental and non-sacred items first. A tilt of the head or a gushing "Ahhhhhhhh" is probably sentiment. Sentimental possessions usually include "should" keep items, like gifts, collectibles, or memorabilia. If an item doesn't elicit a response, it is a number two, and that means it's time to donate or recycle it. There is no room for number twos (or even a number one-and-a-half) in your loved and sacred space.

Take a moment to thoughtfully, deliberately, and with gratitude thank the number twos for being in your life. Release any feelings of loss, sadness, or guilt. It's good to acknowledge why these items came to you and reconcile that they are not useful or loved. Like the adorable 1931 eggbeater from Aunt Judy. Without love, it has to go.

Assess how often something is used. Daily, weekly, or monthly loved items are keepers. Loved items that rarely or never get used do not pass the smell check. A work colleague named Troy dedicated a closet to accessories and rotated loved art as the seasons and his spirit moved. Yes! Experience loved items—don't hide them.

Good self-parenting must be on call to intervene at any moment—you need to be the one who knows what is best for you. Emotionalism can be a vortex of false needs and wants, making your possessions more of an energy suck. Sensitize yourself to items that are energy-giving instead.

As your possessions shrink, your confidence grows. You'll come to realize life goes on and feels incredible without the weight of excess pressing down on you. Eliminating excess unlocks life-giving space both inside your heart and soul. You will literally breathe easier. I promise you, you will utter the words, "Why didn't I do this sooner!"

Take the next few months to parcel through and determine your loved items. Take special notice of the following:

- What became clear while discovering the number ones?

- What delineated a number two?

- How are you stronger?

Choice Tool 2: No Space = No Place

"No Space = No Place" means just that. Space is limited, so use what you have with restraint, creatively and wisely. This choice tool is purely physical. If socks and underwear go in the second drawer of your dresser, which has a maximum capacity of thirteen socks and thirteen pairs of bloomers, then that's it. Period. No cramming. No tugging and cussing when opening the drawer looking for your pink hipsters. What doesn't fit needs to exit stage left. If you are a more logical or pragmatic thinker, this tool might be right for you.

The amount of space we occupy is finite. The $38 billion self-storage industry would not agree with this statement, but in reality, the available square footage in the space you sleep in is limited. Most humans overfill living spaces out of habit, often with things that have little or no use or meaning. This makes us often unable to locate what we do love because it's buried under what we don't love.

This tool is about limit setting and implementing effortless access to your things. Stop tripping over, forgetting about, or digging through meaningless possessions to get at what you love and need. Designate one space where like items can be seen, used, and returned with ease. Spend more time living this glorious life and less time, money, and energy rummaging around crammed and cluttered areas.

The goal:

- Determine *one* location to store like items.

- Establish a satisfactory storage capacity.

- Trim the fat! Eliminate excess. Period.

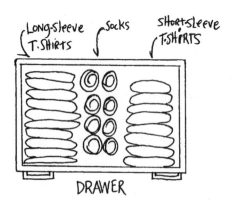

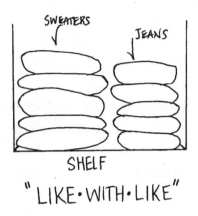

SHELF

" LIKE•WITH•LIKE "

During the dismantling and dispersal phase, you'll form piles of like items (e.g., socks, books, cups, shoes, jackets, etc.), maybe even in front of their final location. The verification that you have too much stuff will quickly become evident.

One Location

Let's start with socks. Consider the perfect storage location where all intimates and socks, including seasonal, holiday, dressy, tights, casual, therapeutic, and sport socks, will be stored. If this location is a drawer, bin, or box, then clear out that one area until it becomes the exclusive intimates and socks spot. Roll or line up each item like slices of bread for optimum visibility, as shown in the image below.

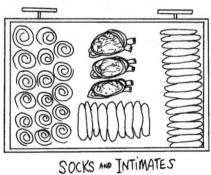

SOCKS AND INTIMATES

Fill every container to a comfortable capacity, one layer deep unless layering identical socks. Piles and cramming are inefficient and not allowed. Logically analyze your use pattern. For example, one pair of feet using, at most, one pair of socks per day equals seven pairs of socks per week. A fourteen-pair storage capacity for socks allows you to do laundry once every two weeks. For our cold weather climates, more socks space may be needed.

Refine your system until the drawers and doors open easily and you're able to achieve visibility to everything at a quick glance. Jeans, shorts, and T-shirts can be stacked on shelves or lined up like slices of bread in drawers the same way as intimates and socks.

If it does not fit, you must omit. Enough said. Making choices based on how things feel, what condition they are in, and frequency of use are helpful criteria to eliminating excess. Run each pair through the love test (is this sock a number one?) or the want vs. need test, which you'll find below, to help you fine-tune your choices.

Tipping Point

Each space has not only a physical capacity, but also a psychological and emotional capacity. When does the space begin to "feel" crowded? Most bodies sense this tipping point when the "too much, closed in, overcrowded" factor has been reached. Test the correct capacity for each drawer, closet, or bookshelf. Start with an empty space and slowly add items. Step back. Sense when the space begins to *feel* full. Add items until you find the correct balance and breathing room for each space.

Shore up the "Goldilocks" version of just right for each drawer, shelf, and countertop. Redefine "full" and "enough." Adherence to new guardrails diminishes tolerance for overcrowded and cluttered spaces. Invariably, you will add new items as time goes on. Remove an item for every new item to maintain this equilibrium between space and stuff. This tool is very pragmatic. Like with like, all in one place. A finite capacity. Boom. That's it.

Choice Tool 3: Need vs. Want

The USA is a full-on, insatiable, consumer-based machine. Marketing professionals are geniuses, conjuring desires we never knew existed, and blurring the line between needs and wants. Like zombies looking for blood, an untethered desire takes control of us. The "Need vs. Want" tool forces you to peel away each want and justify your actual need. Slow down. What do you really *need* to live a full, values-driven life? This tool is a mix of the first two tools but will force the issue of consciousness and personal values. Core personal values and vision inform your need. Ask yourself, "Is the need bringing me closer to or further from my values and vision?" This tool would work for someone who makes choices from both the head and the heart. The sentimental pragmatist.

First understand need. A need is something that is essential to survive. Nutritious food to support the health of our bodies, tools for storing and preparing that food, clean water, a septic system that manages waste and removes disease-causing organisms, good health care, clothing (at least where I live), and a structure that provides shelter and safety to protect us from the elements and intruders are elements that satisfy our basic human needs.

Abraham Maslow (1908–1970) developed a form of psychology called humanistic or positive psychology. The focus is on building a better life, not repairing a broken life. He looked at the whole person, with the belief that all humans want to create a meaningful life. Maslow's Hierarchy of Needs defines five stages of needs, each building on the ladder to reach a self-actualized existence where a person is sharing their unique gifts and experiencing loving companionship. The lower needs must be satisfied before a person can satisfy higher needs. Maslow's Hierarchy of Needs helps navigate need vs. want.

Our physiological needs comprise the lowest level required for our bodies to function properly, like air, food, drink, shelter, clothing, warmth, sex, and sleep.

Safety needs are next, associated with easing our fear of feeling vulner-

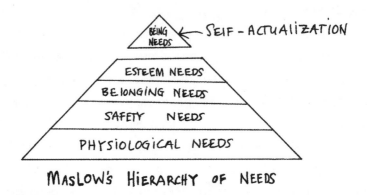

MASLOW'S HIERARCHY OF NEEDS

able in the world. Consider the need for shelter from the elements, a safe home and neighborhood, clothes, a good-paying job, and money in the bank. Rules, order, and limits within our family and society ensure that we feel safe.

The third tier of Maslow's Hierarchy is the need to feel a sense of belonging. We want to be a part of a family, community, a tribe, or personal relationship. Feeling loved and connected to others, a part of something larger, is an important part of being human.

Once our belonging needs are met and we are feeling loved, we feel the need to broaden our impact upon others. Esteem needs allow us to achieve the self-respect that comes from feeling confident, capable, and proud of our accomplishments. We desire a sense of dignity and the freedom and feeling of independence that comes from having a solid reputation. It is at this level that balance between work, family, and others is attained.

The highest tier, self-actualization, is where we find the most peace and long to be our best selves—the most we can be. It's here that we can reach our highest potential, unaffected by the "wants" of society. The self-actualized individual is comfortable in their uniqueness and has a compassionate sense of others. This person notices and appreciates the vast joys, gifts, and experiences life has to offer on the smallest and grandest scale, whether the flight of the hummingbird or the divinity of a healing miracle.

At each level of the hierarchy, we are all striving to live our best possible life. At each level, discord, discomfort, fears, anxiety, stressors, or insecurities naturally exist. Seeking to quell this suffering with material wants is often a reflex. Look deeper. There is a myriad of reasons we acquire stuff. Consider looking at these levels of contentment in your own life. Are possessions a substitute for an emotional or social need?

Do you buy things because you want to feel self-comfort or connected to others? Do you buy clothes because you're insecure about fitting in? When is this cycle ever going to satisfy an emotional need? The stuff will never be enough. Look within, beyond the material items.

Explore your needs using the questions below. Hold each item in your gaze. Access your true connection to each item. Is it frugality, sentimentality, or a reason related to something outside you?

Choosing Based on Need

1. Why is it necessary for survival and safety?

2. What level of need is it satisfying?

3. Am I enough without it?

Yes, this tool is more amorphous, but it is individualized. Learn to separate your emotional connection from your possessions to tease out wants from needs. It's another opportunity to expand good self-parenting skills and deepen your connection to your values and vision with decisions based on need.

Do you need this item to satisfy an emotional or physical need? How does it make you a better person? After you've unraveled the connection to this item, is it a need? If not, it is a want.

Want

Deciphering a need from a want is not an exact science. As a society, we are bombarded by some five thousand advertising messages from the *great and powerful* marketing machines each day. Every form of media tries to tell us we need a newer, bigger, better, faster, more stylish car, shoes, blender, hair dryer, house, phone, or vacuum. We need sleeker styling, quicker picker upping, and buy-one-get-one items that are a must-have *now* because this deal will never come along again—until next week. The art, craft, and science of marketing is utterly fantastic and insidious.

According to Statista, the leader in market and consumer data, the United States is the largest advertising market in the world. We are a wealthy country. We spend a lot of money on things. To attract our attention, the marketing industry spent over $242 billion in 2020. This dollar amount is massive. It's even more tremendous when you consider worldwide spending surpassed $560 billion in 2019. The US is pummeled with advertising, and it shows in our full closets, attics, basements, yards, and garages.

We often construct wants into needs, and they are often endless and insatiable. For example, you are a pretty astute cook with a capable four-burner stove. After coveting a neighbor's six-burner stove, you think about how disappointing your stove is. The want worm grows inside. Life, holidays, spaghetti sauce would be so much better with a six-burner stove. You promise yourself this stove will be the last thing you ask for, and after focused determination and extended credit, it's yours. The stove is everything you had hoped. But are you more "cheffy" than ever? Does the want stop there? I see you looking at your cookware.

When does it end? New season. New shoes. New shoes call for new socks, jacket, handbag, and pants. New cutting boards call for new knives. You will never have enough. Possessing is rooted in desire, habit, pattern, fear, thrift, and sentiment. None of these characterizations deserve prison time, but they do lock us out of a truly richer, freer life. Save your money and live more simply.

Think of deals—clearance, BOGOs, "might need someday" sales—as drugs. When you make purchases unaware of need, your wants contribute to your excess. A drug, I tell you. The various vacuums, rugs, boxes of aluminum foil, sets of dishes, seasonal placemats, tools, magazines, books, water bottles, and towels—whatever the bargain or innocent motivation, the habit or contrived want or need is out of control. A couple dozen rugs are "on hand" when you only ever use your favorite two or three. A drawer full of twist ties when a dozen is plenty. Why? Habit. The beauty is that the cycle can be broken with mindfulness. Take inventory of where you have too much, and know a choice tool is on its way.

Become sensitized to the media barrage for a day, a week, or a month by shutting off the floodgates of advertising. Mute commercials. Don't pick up flyers. Focus on your behavior. Spend no extraneous money for a week. Be proactive. Prepare. Before bed, plan for tomorrow. Coffee at home. Eat homemade meals. Dig into the back of the pantry, fridge, and freezer. Live off your past needs and wants that were "essential." Forgo purchasing food for a while. You're more creative than you think.

The Right Want

A lot of wants are conjured needs—they're all made up. Wants are influenced by outside factors to fulfill a perceived personal deficiency. Wanting to be on trend with clothes, books, wine glasses, or whatever—we simply want to have the *right* thing, at the *right* time, to give it to the *right* person. The time, money, and emotional energy we expend to put all those *rights* together only to have the moment, person, or holiday pass happens more often than nailing it.

Wants are distractors. Let me use an analogy familiar to those of you who live with mosquitos as we do here in Minnesota. Imagine attending a lovely outdoor dinner party on a beautiful summer night. Conversation and wine are flowing as the sun sets. Everyone is focused and engaged. Someone swats one mosquito here and someone else shoos another there. Slowly the focus shifts away from what was a lovely evening of people connecting to a skeeter invasion. Wants are like a horde of distracting mosquitos. And now with the internet, the assault is endless.

What can you do? Take control of your environment. Limit contact with media and influencers. Avoid commercials, forgo picking up magazines, and refrain from unfettered access to the internet. Use the questions below to identify the influences in your life.

1. Where are you vulnerable to the media? Reduce consumption by half.

2. Notice compulsive or obsessive buying? Stop.

3. Look at your credit card and bank statements for the past two months. Calculate how many of your purchases were genuine needs, and how many were simply wants.

Awareness. Awareness. Awareness. Balance. Balance. Balance. Wants will always be present. Strike a better balance between needs and wants to avoid the overdose of either. Need feels nourishing, safe, and loved, and intrinsically enriches your life and living space. You are decluttering because you want a better living space and a better life. Take each decision you make seriously.

Life coaching is built on the premise that introspection and self-honesty will allow you to find your truth. This truth will get you closer to your most authentic self, your truest self. If we listen and answer honestly, we are capable of discerning what is a need and what is a want. The answers reside within. Listen to your truth.

Mistakes

Whatever method you use to make choices, know you will inevitably make mistakes. You will.

In fact, we can survive a mistake and not only face these once-feared emotions, but come out stronger. Xorin Balbes's book *SoulSpace: Transform Your Home, Transform Your Life* discusses the fear of letting go of the wrong possessions, and that in letting go, we will have nothing left. Balbes challenges that belief when he says, "We don't see that holding on keeps us from knowing and experiencing our true natures." This fear of making the wrong choice—or any choice at all—is the same fear that causes the stagnation in our homes. What I have come to know is the fear surrounding the choice is often bigger than the result of the choice.

Expect to learn from mistakes. Be kind and tap into self-compassion. Know you are doing the best you can with what is true today. Making choices is what attacks these heaps and gradually settles frenetic energy for inner peace. Imagine moving easily within, maybe even out of, and into another space one day. A choice made with loving intention will revive and rebalance your life forever.

Determine Choice Tool

In the next chapter you will be using your choice tool(s). Determine which choice tool will work best for you. Practice each tool for a reasonable amount of time. One tool may lose its punch, and that's OK. Try another tool. Take bits and pieces of each tool or find another that shifts the process back into high gear. "Eeny, meeny, miney, mo" is a choice tool. Find one that works and moves stuff out the door.

The ability to choose is a skill that is learned with practice. Below are activities to help you experience choice-making, mistakes, and "do-overs." Know you're building resilience with every choice. Pull your shoulders back, puff your chest, and say with confidence, "I can do this!" Soon you'll make choices more mindfully and instinctively *before* a purchase is ever made.

Activity #1: *Choice Tools*

WHAT: Practice using the three choice tools.

WHY: To determine which choice tool is most effective at eliminating excess for you.

HOW: Find and declutter three areas using each choice tool. Examples where clutter might live include the bedroom closet, pantry, a box in the basement, bathroom closet, T-shirt drawer, a desk, any surface, or the trunk of your car.

TOOLS: Donation bag or box.

TASK: Create one encounter with each of the three choice tools.

- Encounter 1: Love It or Lose It
  - 1. bedroom closet

- Encounter 2: No Space = No Place (mindful of tipping point)
  - 1. bathroom closet

- Encounter 3: Need vs. Want
  - 1. junk drawer

TIME: Fifteen minutes per encounter.

Reflection Activity

WHAT: What tool worked best? Why?

: In the space below, answer the reflection questions.

Activity #2: *Clothing That Reflects an Authentic Self*

Every choice you make feeds your vision of self and home. You have to be comfortable with your choices. To me it's like finding clothes that fit. Adjusting, fidgeting, or lacking confidence in our clothing stinks. When clothes fit, feel, and function right, our best self shines and we're able to be more present and authentic.

WHAT: Imagine, then collage an outfit of your dreams. Money is no object.

WHY: An authentic outfit translates to an authentic home.

HOW: Search online or in magazines, or draw clothing types that represent you.

TOOLS: Computer or tablet. Magazines. Sheet of paper. Glue or tape. Drawing and coloring utensils.

TASK: Create a collage, compile accessories, shoes, scarves, hats, jackets, undergarments, etc. that reflect your authentic self.

TIME: One hour.

Reflection Activity

WHAT: How would you alter your vision of home to include these elements of your authentic self?

: In the space below, answer the reflection question.

"Excellence is never an accident. It is always the result of high intention, sincere effort, and intelligent execution; it represents the wise choice of many alternatives—choice, not chance, determines your destiny."
ARISTOTLE

See your ideal life and home becoming clearer with every choice you make. Shed possessions so your dream space and most divine self have enough room to appear.

♩

"This Is Me"
Keala Settle

7 | Dismantle and Disperse

"Nothing will work unless you do."
MAYA ANGELOU

Finally, we begin the "ass and elbows" work of decluttering. Dismantle and disperse means you're moving excess either out the door or to a vision-worthy location. By now, you've acknowledged actions that have contributed to the mess and willingly taken responsibility to command and control it. You've embraced a few key values, captured a hope-filled vision, and bolstered resilience through discomfort. With a fuller toolbox, we're ready to charge forward, fully fueled with motivation to remove stuff with clarity and discernment.

Dismantle

Dismantle means to take apart. For decluttering, that means to dig into one closet, drawer, box, or pile at a time, so you can gain complete visibility of what you own in entirety. Item by item. All your pots and pans, pens, shoes, shovels, shirts, and so on need to be in one spot so you can review and begin to make choices. Marie Kondo, the author of *The Life-Changing Magic of Tidying Up,* does a beautiful job illuminating this to her clients by taking everything a person owns in a certain category, like clothing for example, and piling it onto one surface. Everyone is astounded by how much they possess. Seeing in totality is crucial to eliminating the denial that shrouds decluttering success and of course excess itself.

Disperse

Dispersal is the act of collecting and moving *like items* to what will be the best, most accessible, logical location in our loved living space, according to our individual lifestyle and vision. All socks go in one place, all shoes in another, crafts, magazines, and pet toys each categorized in their best place. We'll collect hats and summer sandals from the hall closet, basket, or shelf, and move them to one final resting place. Multiple locations can expand inventory unnecessarily. Keeping like items in one location tempers unnecessary accumulation because you know what you have.

Immediately after dismantling an area, disperse like items in *one* final, efficient, most convenient resting spot. These combined actions reveal the full picture of what you own in each category one space, closet, box, bin, or drawer at a time.

Like with like. A simple mantra. Key to managing everything. Place shoes with shoes, books with books, towels with towels, linens with linens, screwdrivers with screwdrivers, photos with photos, collectibles with like collectibles, and so on. Yes, I know this isn't always possible, but limit the exceptions, or clutter will grow.

With the tools you've collected, you have the ability to assess from the first touch which items deserve to live in your sacred space, as well as what leaves and who gets it. Masterfully and mindfully plug unnecessary items into your to-go list, with an exit plan and giving plan at the ready. Corners, cabinets, and closets will declutter more easily because of undeterred soul-centered personal values, an undimmable vision, burgeoning confidence, courage, determination, resilience, and compassion for yourself and others.

The beauty is after *this* layer of decluttering is complete, the remaining prized pieces are those that embody your steadfastly held vision. Chapter 8: Vision Actualized uses those pieces to assist as you design, arrange, and organize your space to bring that vision to life. So exciting! I can't wait for you to come home!

> *"Before anything else, preparation is the key to success."*
> **ALEXANDER GRAHAM BELL**

Decluttering Plan

The doing of decluttering, dismantle and disperse, is sequential and demands a plan. You will create and prioritize a project list. A prioritized list becomes your decluttering plan. Your priority list is your GPS through decluttering to your destination, your vision. When you know what you are doing, you won't get distracted, overwhelmed, or frustrated. Little projects and manageable goals will help you maintain focus one proficient project at a time. If you've never experienced the exhilaration of checking things off a list, this process will prove to be supremely rewarding. With optimism remember that every minute of every project is getting you closer to your end goal.

Marathon

Tackling any project takes conviction, sharpened focus, continued effort, and dedication to the end goal. I had "run a marathon" on my bucket list since I was a teenager. Well, at thirty-seven, I found myself sitting alone in my house, newly single, other projects completed, with wonderful friends, a great job, and nothing to really occupy my free time. I realized this was a luxury and would be a great time to train for my bucket list marathon. I assessed my situation: my soft and squatty body and the fact I was a smoker made this dream seem somewhat improbable. At five feet tall I would have to take two steps for every step of an "average" person. I could have decided to keep doing the same thing and simply cross it off my list forever. But I wanted to quit hoping and smoking and finally do it!

I researched novice marathon training programs that required running a few miles each week to start, because looking at the peak week forty-mile training regimen seemed improbable and insurmountable. Although I was an enthusiastic athlete in school and life, I was not a runner. The novice runner training plan said I could successfully run a marathon in eighteen weeks. So I quit smoking, bought shiny new running shoes and a good bra, taped my training schedule to my mirror, and began. I moved forward trusting this reliable program, committing to the time and effort recommended and believing in my dream.

The plan as a whole overwhelmed me, so I chose to focus on one week's training at a time, mentally absorbing what seemed like manageable mileage goals, and physically doing the work with welcomed days of rest. The training program, as it turned out, was the most amazing, meditative, peaceful, and empowering part of the marathon experience. Each week I grew in stamina and strength, exhilarated by the goals I accomplished, which had initially seemed overwhelming.

The marathon training was fun and to this day is still one of my most transformational accomplishments. I did something I never imagined possible. The medal I received that day means little. What I carry with me still is how empowered I still feel by doing the little things every day that made this dream a reality. Decluttering is also a marathon. Slow, steady, planned progress daily that leads to accomplishing something one thought insurmountable. Yes. You. Can.

How will you set your plan and yourself up to succeed? If something didn't work, *do something* differently. What do you have to lose but an old, unreliable habit? If all you have tolerance for is tackling one shelf in the medicine cabinet, that's totally great. So be it. Build grit one shelf, one micro-project at a time. The project size and scope you can handle will inform your project list. Break everything down into manageable chunks. Let's launch into creating your decluttering project list.

PROJECT MANAGEMENT
Creating a Project List
Transformation is defined as a thorough and dramatic change. Decluttering is a transformation. It enlists our personal repeated effort while maintaining a determined and narrow focus and eventually bearing witness to the metamorphosis both internally and externally, with the end goal of creating a loved and functional home. A project list is the critical means through transformation to this glorious end.

In my cleaning business I learned to break down a twenty-five-room house into bite-sized pieces. This helped me make big projects feel more manageable and less overwhelming. You too must learn to break down and prioritize a project into smaller bites. Know where you will start and what comes next and next and next until the project is complete. Any space (bedroom, living room, garage, etc.) can be broken down into smaller bite-sized pieces. For example:

Bathroom:

a) Medicine cabinet

b) Vanity top

c) Vanity cabinet

d) Linen cabinet

e) Tub/Shower

f) Étagère

g) Floor

h) Walls

Dining room:

a) Table—on and under might be two projects

b) Hutch—on and in drawers might be two projects

c) Linens—Multiple locations might mean multiple projects

d) Other stacks in corners

e) Floor

f) Walls

On this page or on a separate piece of paper break your bathroom or dining room down into smaller bite-sized pieces or projects. Once identified, you can determine how to approach or begin each project. A project list is great, but knowing where to start can be a major roadblock. Knowing where to start and how to work through any project is key. Below are some ways to approach a project.

Stand in front of your bathroom or dining room. Read through the various ways to approach any project. Imagine yourself tackling this project using one of these approaches.

How to Approach a Project

1. Divide the space into sections, halves, or quarters. Tackle one section at a time.

2. Start at one wall and move from one wall to the next.

3. Top-Down: Start at the top of one surface or drawer and progress down. Repeat to the next surface.

4. Bottom-Up: Start at floor level and work up from there.

In the illustration below, think about clearing out a closet either from the top down or the bottom up. The top image is cluttered. The lower image is decluttered. Take this project on at home. Have bins ready to separate into donate, sell, or move piles as you remove items to maintain order.

The figure below is an example of a dismantling project list. Simply make a list of all the rooms, nooks, crannies, and spaces you need to declutter. No need to have any particular order of importance. You will prioritize this project list later. For now, there are no right or wrong projects.

Create the project list systematically and methodically. Again, maintaining a sense of order will reduce confusion. Below are suggested ways to create a project list for your entire home.

1. Top-Down: top floors to lower floors. Attic to basement.

2. Bottom-Up: lower level to upper levels. Basement to attic.

3. High-use (bathrooms or kitchens) to low-use (guest room or patio) areas or vice versa.

4. Biggest rooms to smallest rooms and vice versa.

5. Least overwhelming to most overwhelming spaces.

6. Front door to back door.

Develop your project list using one of the above suggested methods. Use the empty Project List below.

Project List	
Location	Project & Goal

Below is a sample of a project list with associated goals for a living space that begins at a front door and culminates at the back door.

Sample Project List	
Location	Project & Goal
1. Entry closet	Donate unused coats, shoes, boots, hats, etc. Goal: create space for guest coats.
2. Half bathroom	Remove wallpaper and paint walls
3. Hallway closet	Donate unused games, puzzles, and blankets
4. Living room	Replace sofa with sectional. Add storage.
5. Dining room and hutch	Remove unwanted china and linens

6. Kitchen	Clear out rarely used cups, dishes, and utensils
7. Bedroom and closet	Remove everything from under bed
8. Full bathroom	Properly dispose of unused medication
9. Back entry	Install shoe cabinet

In this sample, your project list contains nine projects. Next, prioritize your most important to least important projects. Where will you begin? Maybe you want to begin with the easiest project which is, as shown above, the hallway closet, or you choose the Top-Down approach. These are *absolutely* essential project management tools. A plan, a goal, a priority, and an approach to begin. With your vision in tow, you'll start to pull everything off the top shelf. Loved items that will stay go in one pile. No longer wanted items go in the donate/give pile. Stuff that is in the wrong place goes into another pile. Next, remove items that are hanging and move them to the floor. In each case, determine what will be kept, donated, or moved. Put keepers back into the closet, careful to maintain breathing room and order. Remove donated items and move keeper items from the "move" pile to their proper location. Repeat for your next project.

Removing items from their old locations and dispersing them to their new locations will be a methodical mess. Things do look worse during this chapter, but if project progress continues, this mess will be temporary. Yes, you're adding stuff to already stuffed areas. Without the project list, you will quit. This I will guarantee. Take yourself seriously. You are a project manager, so tackle each project like a project manager. Use your project list and a thoughtful approach, and follow through to completion on each project before starting another one. Stay focused on *one mess at a time*. Put your blinders on to avoid getting overwhelmed and distracted. I am confident you will masterfully manage these new yet fleeting messes.

Project List Prioritization

A project list is absolutely necessary. The mind can so easily ping-pong back and forth with conflicting ideas on where to start and what to do next without a plan. Prioritizing puts those ping-pong balls in a line and tells the mind which "mess ball" to pick up and focus on now. When that mess ball is complete, go back and pick up another prioritized project until all the mess balls are gone.

Use your project list to create your priority list. This priority list is your to-do list and methodically plans your entire decluttering process. Having trouble prioritizing? Use the questions below to identify the first ping-pong ball you will pick up. Each ping-pong ball is a project. Use the blank priority list below to write project priorities. Come back to this list of questions whenever you are at a standstill or need a new project idea.

- Instinctively what rooms are you most drawn to?

_____

- Where are you most eager to see results?

_____

- Where do you spend the most or least amount of time?

_____

- If accommodating guests is important, which spaces are critical?

_____

- Which project or space feels most manageable?

_____

- When completed, which area would feel most rewarding?

_____

- Which project is most closely linked to your values?

_____

- Which project most feeds your vision?

_____

Priority List			
Room or Area	Priority	Approach	Time

Consider prioritizing one project that will bring a sense of accomplishment. Review your approaches to each area and document what worked or didn't work for you. The approach can vary by project, or you might find one method fits your style over others. You are learning, so be flexible. Remember you are more creative and resourceful than you think. You are also building your tolerance and grit with each project.

Set a date. When will you begin the first priority project?

The first priority is all you have to focus on. Keep track of how much time this project takes. Recording duration of a project will allow you to gauge the length of future projects.

Decluttering Tools

Now that you have a project priority, be prepared to dismantle. Collect moving and storing tools. As stuff is moving around in your space, some or all tools listed below may be helpful. Resist buying any new tools. Diligently look through the stuff you already have or use creative substitutes.

- Boxes, bins, baskets, or bags of varying sizes

- Recycling containers for quick disposal

- Duct tape

- Trash can or bags

- Measuring tape

- Scissors, utility knife, or another sharp knife

- Office supplies: paper clips, a marker, another writing utensil, file folders, notepad, sticky notes

- Access to a shredder

- Step stool or ladder

Place extra bins, extra shelving, and usable boxes in one central location. Dedicate one location to extra tools and storage containers so they can be easily accessed during decluttering. These will be used to store donations, to store items that need fixing, or to move like items from place to place.

Place a note on the wall to remind yourself this is an intentional work zone. Hard hats optional.

Where is that space?

_____

Declutter—Dismantle and Disperse

You are ready. As you touch each item, decide where it should live according to your vision. The mantra "touch it once and decide" is a great rule of thumb. Set a goal to remove a certain percentage of stuff during each work session. A 20 percent reduction is two items gone out of ten. Three out of ten is 30 percent, six out of ten is 60 percent. Set your percentage goal. Stick with this percentage for several decluttering sessions. See how it feels. Adjust as needed. This is *your* process.

Write down the percentage of excess you will commit to get rid of during each decluttering session. I commit to getting rid of _____ percent.

Dispersal

Clarify what qualifies as a perfect location. Consult your vision. Ask yourself:

- Where will this be when my space is perfect?

- Where will I likely look for this when I need it?

- Where will this item be used most often?

- How can I make this item accessible and convenient to grab and return?

Final locations may shift and change. No worries. This is practice, a deliberate yet fluid way of managing the movement of your stuff.

Label each container:

- Contents

- Final destination

- Additional descriptions as needed

Label your boxes and don't overfill them. The container should be easy to close. Transport labeled boxes (visible on two sides) to their final destination. Add specific content information and a reminder of where the items came from to help spark your memory. Careful not to pile the boxes so high they compromise personal safety or the integrity of the contents.

Again, spaces will appear worse before they look better. What differentiates the new mess is that this time, the chaos is ordered and intentional. With diligence, the chaotic phase will not last. Consistent signage, a clear process, and steady progress will manage the disarray and eventually bring order. Consistency in new behaviors will help break old, destructive behaviors. Repetitively altering old patterns in this process will lead to successfully limiting excess in the future. Who wants to go through this mess again?!

The Black Hole—"Fix Me!" Items

A "Fix me" item is anything you have kept, saying, "I am going to fix that!" But you haven't done so. Now is the moment to be honest and realistic. Due to barriers like time, money, knowing who to call, buying the right tool, finding the missing part or the right space, or all of the above, fixing this thing hasn't been a priority. What is *different* now that makes you believe you will fix it? Be honest.

Hey, if you have no barriers to repairing it, then place this project on your priority list and get it done. Schedule the repair on your calendar. Take action on finding the part, the tool, the space, the money, or the time to fix it. But if you haven't fixed it within two months, these things are now called "broken" and need to be recycled and removed. Going forward, set a two month "fix it" timeline. Date the item. Repair or remove it after the timeline expires. This is exactly how clutter creeps back into your space and your life. Don't hesitate. Don't ignore.

Be Decisive. Move On.

The length of this chapter is short. The duration of dismantling, dispersing, and decision-making is up to you. Now is the time to use your choice tools, activate your giving plan, and get stuff out the door. This is the chapter when you are making decisions and doing the heavy lifting of decluttering. Moving and removing, baby!

Here are a few strategies to accelerate the decluttering process:

- Make decisions in bulk or with broad strokes.

- Don't touch every item. Touch the keepers.

- Two bins of old rags? Keep a dozen.

- A ten-year magazine collection? Pull out the top two per year.

- Garage full of shovels and rakes? Pick two sturdy and versatile options of each.

Set limits by focusing on need and available space. *If* space is available, sprinkle in some wants.

Forty pairs of shoes and four hundred books to narrow down? Where is the one space these shoes and books will live? The space available is your guardrail. If fifteen pairs and three shelves of books are what's available, so be it. New stuff gets to come in, but old stuff will need to leave. This discipline will establish a beautiful equilibrium.

There is no perfect way to get rid of stuff. Stop overthinking. The item has a functional purpose or it doesn't. Put this thing to use or get rid of it. Shed the shackles of should. Others need your stuff. Be the joy bringer.

Consistency in new behaviors will help break old behaviors. Anything new takes time to integrate. Similar to breaking down big tasks into achievable components, you can do the same with changing your behavior. Incorporate one small project management skill at a time. Over time this skill will transform into a behavior change for good, forever.

I have struggled to find my ideal weight for years. I found Mary, a petite powerhouse health coach who, among offering many great ideas, helped me see that small and consistent behavior changes over time help anyone reach any goal.

Mary introduced me to Jeff Olsen's "slight edge" concept in his book, The Slight Edge, to help me lose ten pounds. Both Mary and Jeff fiercely believe it's the small choices we make each day, that over time make all the difference. I am more mindful to skip the elevator and take the stairs, choose a salad over fries, or always choose to drink another glass of water. I am not perfect, but I know these small changes make a difference.

Any focused effort, even the slightest incremental and consistent positive change, helps when you do it day in and day out. This consistency can make any vision a reality. Saving for a new sofa at a few dollars a week seems like it would take a lifetime. Trent Hamm from The Simple Dollar suggests that saving steadily, one dollar week one, two dollars week two, three dollars week three, and so on for fifty-two weeks would glean $1,378.00. Small steps toward any goal are rewarded.

Managing clutter is similar. Simple, conscious choices like putting the coffee cup in the dishwasher, putting today's clothes away today, and tossing today's junk mail today will be noticed, especially when you do them over and over. The space around you changes. You will feel so much better about yourself and your space because the space around you will look and feel better too. A little positive effort each day is rewarded in results.

This book has been a case of investing small chunks of time for over a decade, while my infant daughter napped and marched through elementary and middle school. Between house moves, job changes, major home repairs, and life's distractions, it was my ability to get back on track after falling away from the habit that continued to result in progress. I was never willing to give up. This book is the evidence of continuous effort over (a long) time. I couldn't give up and I don't like to write. You may not like to declutter, but please, never give up. This will all be worth it.

In time, you'll relish the reward of crossing completed projects off the list. Even if lists have failed to be rewarding in the past, I hope this time is different. Celebrate the act of crossing things off your to-do list. Focus. Finish. Repeat. Cheers and tiny high fives!

Continue to pull from the project list and add to the priority list as items are crossed off. Each item you touch and move promotes progress and propels you closer to your goal. Focus on what *is* getting done, not what needs to be done. Revisit the values and vision work you did previously to give you a boost of energy as often as needed. Stay committed and focused. Above all, keep moving.

Help Is an Option
Decluttering is a taxing job. You need energy to gather momentum and stay focused and motivated. The physical demands of schlepping things hither and yon has to come from somewhere. What is your modus operandi as a project manager? Review your prior work habits from the past. What do you do well and where are your roadblocks? Are you slow to start? Do you go hard and peter out after a few hours? Where are you decisive? What will you avoid?

Be honest. What tasks do you do well? Where do you falter or get stuck?

I am great at _____

I get stuck when _____

What would help look like for you to really do things differently this time? If you had a genie in a bottle and were given three decluttering "Help!" wishes, in what three areas would you most need or want help? Write your help wishes below:

1. _____

2. _____

3. _____

We all shine in different lights. Help can come in many forms. Whether you're paying for help or not, consider an accountability partner for those less ambitious moments. An accountability partner is a check-in partner. They keep you on track and moving through your project with a daily or weekly planned call or text.

An accountability partner could be a key to success throughout the decluttering process. Consider someone or a company who shines where you don't, and allow them to be the shoulder that busts through barriers, and a loving, fun, and firm presence. Someone who believes in your vision quest and has time to help. What is not helpful is someone who convinces you to keep things you are working so hard to get rid of. Below is a list of some qualities that make a successful accountability partner:

Challenges me	Organized
Consistent	Patient
Easy to talk to	Pleasing temperament
Good work ethic	Reliable
Honest	Respectful
Loving	

You can find an accountability partner in a friend or family member, or search for a local organizer or clutter cleanup specialist online or in your local paper. Does anyone come to mind as a good accountability partner or helper? Anyone you find should be vetted, especially if you don't already know them. Check references and reviews. Trust is built over time. Keep in mind that free help is of no help if the time you spend together is distracting and unproductive.

Fun

Stay motivated and have fun. The right mood enhancement can make any decluttering project more enjoyable. What simple pleasures spark energy and make you smile? Place your vision in your work space to remember why you are doing this in the first place.

What makes you smile and feel energized? Below are a few examples:

- Music

- Special (non-alcoholic) beverage

- Favorite, comfy clothes

- Sunlight

- Reward at intervals or when finished

- Crossing projects off the list

Recall a time when you tackled a difficult project. What made that project successful? What can you duplicate in this project? Sometimes time is the most important ingredient of any project.

Time

Dedication of time, a most precious resource to decluttering, is essential. Flesh out your available decluttering hours each day and week.

What is your available time to devote to decluttering?

Hours per day: _____

Hours per week: _____

Days of the week:_____

Add this information to your calendar. Set a schedule that is realistic and action-oriented.

Time is precious. So is motivation. Progress is pushing stuff out the door and that comes from dogged, consistent effort.

Accountability Activities

The following activities provide opportunities for small successes. This "save a nickel a day" mentality will get you to your vision one small project at a time. Who doesn't like to feel like a winner? The feeling expands confidence. The two activities below are opportunities to learn that progress using small projects, consistent methodology, and incremental changes can lead to monumental change and continue to engage you in the decluttering process, thereby building tolerance to being uncomfortable.

Activity #1: *Small Project Management*

Being a project manager simply means you get shit done. The learning will be repeatable for larger projects.

WHAT: Complete three small scale dismantle and disperse projects.

WHY: Create an efficient and repeatable process.

HOW: Identify three small clutter problems. Possible examples:

o   Too many undergarments (Many never used, ripped, or uncomfortable)

o   Junk drawer is out of control (No divided spaces, duplicates, or wrong location)

o   Too many household plants (Visual clutter. Many overgrown, unhealthy, or in the wrong location)

o   Daily mail gets buried and ignored (Inconsistent location of mail and drop area)

o   Coats aren't hung up (No rules or noncompliance, no hooks or hangers, no consequences)

o   Too many coffee mugs (No space, sentiment over space, many unused)

o   Other…

TOOLS: Paper. Writing utensil. Consult decluttering tools list on page 174.

TASK: Write down the project or problem and suggested approach. De-clutter (dismantle and disperse) three small clutter problem areas.

TIME: Thirty minutes per project problem. Ninety minutes total.

Reflection Activity

WHAT: What project was the most successful? Why?

: In the space below, answer the reflection questions.

_____

_____

_____

_____

_____

_____

_____

Activity #2: *Practice Percentage Purging*

WHAT: Create opportunities to practice purging a percentage of stuff.

WHY: Boosts analytical skills.

HOW: Create three purging projects. Examples below.

o   Your handbag or wallet

o   A shelf in the pantry, bathroom, bedroom, or garage

o   A drawer, dresser, or any closet

TASK: In each project remove 5 percent. Replace. Then 25 percent. Replace. Then 50 percent of excess in each project. Get rid of a percentage of your choosing.

TOOLS: One bin to disperse excess or process through giving plan.

TIME: Fifteen minutes per project. Forty-five minutes for three projects.

Reflection Activity

WHAT: What percentage were you most uncomfortable purging?

: In the space below, answer the reflection question.

_____

_____

_____

_____

_____

_____

_____

I was once an interior painter. The prep work was 80 percent of the job at times. I had to set up a solid project plan and prioritize everything on that plan, starting with collecting and purchasing paint and materials, including the tape, tarps, ladders, plastic, scrapers, and hole-filling mud. I needed to assess how the project would be approached and manage my time, all before I put a drop of paint on the wall. Successful planning delivers successful decluttering. Do the prep work, work your plan, be consistent, and you will sail through decluttering. You *will* actualize your dream space.

"Up & Up"
Coldplay

8 | Vision Actualized

"When you visualize, then you materialize."
DENIS WAITLEY

The decluttering work of dismantling, dispersing, and deciding has been done. Your number ones, your many "Yes!" treasures, all things you need and love now have the space to shine. In this chapter, we will take keeper items and basic design principles, arranging and organizing them to showcase the marriage of function and beauty. We will usher and move these pieces like a puzzle to create your loved home. I am giddy with excitement for you.

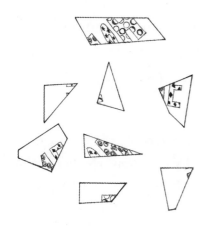 

Actualizing a vision is a project, albeit the most fun project ever! By now, I hope it's no surprise that this project needs a plan and this final plan is called a *design plan*. The design plan includes furniture placement to maximize comfort and movement of people and pets. We want every soul who enters your space to feel cared for, supported, and loved. We want you to be able to live freely and fully as yourself in this space. This plan counts on the project manager—you—to recognize when enough is enough, and relies on your restraint and boundaries to keep chaos at bay. A balance of order and functional aesthetic will allow your unique personality to be illuminated.

"Balance is not something you find, it's something you create."
JANA KINGSFORD

Design Tools

Design tools will bring new skills meant to turn on an open mind that enlivens possibilities. Continue to cultivate a willingness to perceive fresh ideas for furniture placement to open up traffic patterns or discover diverse ways of using pieces. For example, a bookcase or a sofa floating in a room can create two spaces where once there was one.

The following five design tools will bring to light your sacred vision:

Each of these individual tools can unlock personal creativity and help achieve balance in each space, all in service of your vision. The five "Fs" are each a layer to contribute ideas and set parameters and guidelines as you continue to cull through what will and won't work in each space. Maintain an objective view of each living space to help you actualize a design that not only looks good, but also showcases your unique vision and serves its guests.

> *"You can't use up creativity. The more you use, the more you have."*
> **MAYA ANGELOU**

A lot has changed because of you. You tapped into your courage and found grit and fortitude, many times through frustration. You demonstrated strength at every challenge. Because of this and so much heavy lifting, your clutter has already diminished. I am in awe of the mountain that you have moved to get to this point.

I admire and acknowledge the enormity of work you have done and are doing to get to this stage. You are in the last three miles of a marathon, which too has its challenges. You are tired and excited at the same time. This compounded resilience will carry you across the finish line. Remember where you started. Revel in your progress. You are so close to the finish line yourself.

Bring Everything to the Party

Review your vision storyboard, top three values, and the art of choosing. All the skills you have accumulated throughout the decluttering process will be called upon during this vision creation phase. Refining is easier now because of all you have accomplished. This mama is proud of you. If each skill were a badge on a fancy sash, I hope you would wear it proudly. You deserve to feel the confidence that comes from working so hard.

Restraint

As you practice each design tool of function, focus, fit, feel, and fun, I ask you to pause and live with changes for a few days or weeks before you determine what is working or not working. It's easy to react negatively when a change is new. Practice restraint. Use the resilience you've gained to consider only current possessions. Don't buy anything new. Wait with want. If something isn't working, don't rush out to make a new purchase right away. Fully articulate the problem. Look around your current spaces to find something that might fulfill your need or want. Be clear about what is needed, then patiently hunt for the right something. Don't settle.

Go through the five "Fs" in each space before purchasing anything new. Do *not* rush out and buy organizing gizmos. Tap into the space where extra bins, shelving, and boxes have been stored to find suitable storage and organization solutions that will work for now. Wait until you have moved through 80 to 100 percent of your possessions before purchasing anything new. Cleaned take-out containers, vases, jars, and cutout tissue boxes make great storage options for now (or for always). Decorate (or not) their exteriors with wrapping paper, colorful tape, or spray paint. The personalized touch may bring you smiles and satisfaction.

Activities are interspersed throughout this chapter to get you comfortable with these design tools that may be new to you. This may also be a playground you have long wanted to come back to. Wherever you are on your design journey, these are the tools that will manifest your vision. These activities help you move from an image to reality.

To get started, make a list of all your living spaces. Start at the entrance to your space. Every hallway with or without a closet, every doorway that leads to a space, and every room should be given a name and put on this list. I am sitting in a sweet apartment right now that is one open living space with two doorways. One leads to a *bathroom* and the second to the *mechanical room*. This 400-square-foot space has an open *kitchen, living room,* and *eating space* and a three-quarter wall separating the *bedroom*. My living space list would include six separate rooms. If needed, make a list of your separate rooms or spaces here.

------------------------------   ------------------------------   ------------------------------

------------------------------   ------------------------------   ------------------------------

------------------------------   ------------------------------   ------------------------------

------------------------------   ------------------------------   ------------------------------

Function

The function of something is its intended use. A belt can serve a couple purposes. It can hold up pants, hold up a bumper, add color and style to an outfit, or all of these and then some. The function of a space has to do with the activities done in this space. How will each space be used? What is the purpose of each particular living space? Will people sleep, eat, watch TV, read, entertain, tend to bodily functions, park a car, work, game, or craft in this space? How a space is used will inform the room's function or purpose. The function is important because it will determine the furnishings and accessories needed. A sleeping space needs a bed of some sort. Eating spaces need tables and chairs.

A space can serve multiple functions, and the furnishings need to take that into consideration. A bedroom or a kitchen might do double duty as an office.

A living room may function as a craft area, a guest room as an office or TV room.

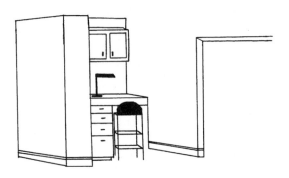

The furniture and accessories will account for and support each unique need. The large cabinet in this bedroom can store clothing, office supplies, and bedding.

All the surfaces (shelves, benches, or tables) and storage areas (cabinets, drawers, baskets, closets, and storage ottomans) can be creatively utilized to serve multiple functions. To be functional, items like knitting yarn, magazines, books, games, movies, or hats must be easily accessible, or the function will fail. Create the right functional solutions, or stuff will inevitably create the unsightly piles or messes you have been trying so hard to clean up.

The following activity is an immersive understanding of function unique to you. Each living space serves to satisfy a purpose or an activity. Once you understand the function(s) of each space, then you will pull furnishings together, filling each space with your needed and loved stuff in a way that fulfills your dream and vision.

Function Activity

WHAT: From your list of rooms in your space, brainstorm likely activities for each living space. Add items needed to support these activities. If an activity can occur in multiple spaces, determine the *best* place for the activity.

WHY: Clearly identifying what happens where ensures proper furniture, accessories, and discipline, which helps maintain order.

HOW: Use the function list and function/needs forms below to plan how each space will be used.

TOOLS: Function list. Function/needs form. Writing utensil. Paper. Computer or tablet.

TASK: List each space, the function(s) it will serve, and items needed to fulfill that function.

TIME: Two hours.

Function List

TV	Guest room	Hobbies
Computer	Storage	Reading
Gaming	Meals	Exercising
Sleep	Children	Socializing
Study	Teens	Pets
Work	Elders	Other?
Office	Crafts	

- o Who will be using this space? Think number of kids, pets, teens, adults, or groups to accommodate daily or on special occasions.

- o What are all the activities to consider in this space, and what furniture will support those functions? For example, TV: watching, seating, gaming; sleeping: bed; reading: seating, lighting, bookcase; eating: table, chairs, storage; working: desk, chair, lamp, etc.

- o How will specific furniture or accessories you already have be used in this space?

FUNCTION/NEEDS		
Space	Function	Needs
Living room	TV watching. Cozy reading	Comfortable seating: ottoman, reading material, lamp
Bedroom	Sleep. Store clothes	Bed. Dresser: five drawers or more

Reflection Activity

WHAT: What was the biggest realization about function and need that surfaced as a result of this activity?

: In the space below, answer the reflection question.

_____

_____

_____

_____

_____

_____

_____

Focus

The focus simply asks, "What should I be looking at?" Focus showcases what is most special or most important in this space, and furniture is generally directed toward that attention-getter. Does your room center around a television, fireplace, or amazing architectural details? Is the focal point a buffet, large windows, a beautiful view, or an incredible bed with a unique headboard? Art, family heirlooms, and your number one treasure(s) can be showcased and provide a focus.

When someone walks into a space, what do you want them to notice? People need to have something to do with their eyes, and psychologically, they want and need to know what goes on in each space so they can relax. Together the function and focus help people understand the purpose of a space.

Be careful with focus. Less is more. If you highlight *every* treasure, nothing stands out. When everything is important, nothing is important. For example, choose a couple precious, quirky, or similar items in one prominent spot. Love the color green? Emphasize your favorite color in a few accessories or one larger piece, but too many green things in a space and the emphasis is lost.

Explore and select your *most* important treasure to focus on. Allow this piece to be the start of a story. One powerful statement along with little connections to that story can continue throughout other living spaces. The image below begs to have furnishings oriented around the fireplace: a cozy conversation area with a couple chairs and a sofa where friends or family can gather.

Questions to determine the focus of each space:

- What is the *most* important activity in this space?

- Any furniture or architecture to highlight?

- Large walls? Use wall art or dramatic paint color to create a focal point.

- A fireplace, dining room table, or bed are natural focal points.

- Rugs on floors or a wall also make a great focal point.

- Who is meant to be using this space? If it's a kid's play space, what will draw kids in?

Multiple Focal Points

Sometimes it's hard to define one main focal point of a room. Remember, if everything is important, nothing is important. Experiment. Make a decision. Design the space around choice one. Live with this decision for a week or two. Your ability to articulate the most important thing in the room establishes great ground rules and boundaries. Be mindful; if you have multiple activities going on in a space, you need room for furnishings and accessories to support those activities.

Fit

The function and focus are becoming clearer. Now we need to address how the possessions related to your vision actually fit in each space. This is where the rubber meets the road. What pieces are needed for the activities in this space and where will they be placed? Is there sufficient room to easily move around and through the space? Just like with the work you did to see what will actually fit in drawers, in cabinets, and on shelves, remember, "If it doesn't fit, you must omit!"

While refining your space, keep these considerations in mind:

1. Focal point of the space

2. Physical size of furniture pieces

3. Furniture and accessories to support activities

4. Traffic patterns

Use these four considerations as guardrails. Don't overfill a space. Find other places where pieces might be useful. If needed go back to chapter six and use the tools to make choices or use your giving plan. Thoughtful order and organization will maximize fit. Below, the function/needs tool has been expanded to include fit. You have already determined function and needs. Now, reality sets in as you measure item(s) for *fit* within each space.

FUNCTION/NEEDS/FIT			
Space	Function	Needs	Fit
Living room	TV watching. Cozy reading	Comfortable seating: ottoman, reading material, lamp	
Bedroom	Sleep. Store clothes	Bed. Dresser: five drawers or more	

There are two options to find out if you have the right furniture in each space.

1. Create a scale drawing on paper: measure each room and the furniture intended for each space on paper first before lifting any furniture.

2. Gather some strong backs and move the furniture hither and yon to find the best fit.

Option two requires brawn to move furnishings—and don't forget the pizza and beverages if you ask friends for help. It also risks potential damage to pieces while you're moving them around.

Option one, creating a scale drawing, is "shrinking" the space and furniture proportionally onto a standard piece of paper. Mildly mind-blowing and possibly overwhelming I realize, but hang in here with me. The art of a scale drawing is a tool that expands your creative and pragmatic mind. This might help: picture your round coffee table the size of a dime. Now move that dime around on a piece of paper. I will teach you how to draw a miniaturized room including little paper furniture cutouts to practice placing furniture in your space.

Why? Scale drawings of your space and furnishings are beneficial for four reasons:

1. Confirm furniture pieces actually fit—without physically moving them.

2. Better understand traffic patterns in the room.

3. Develop an ability to visualize your dream space.

4. Full-scale drawing with furniture laid out will help communicate your plan when your moving buddies show up. Any size, flow, or function problems are made clear and can be solved

moving paper furniture without back-breaking effort of physically moving real furniture.

Do you envision a cozy reading nook? The scale drawing of the space and desired furniture will allow pieces to be moved within a room or from room to room effortlessly. Knowledge of a quiet space to house reading materials, a chair, and an outlet for a lamp can be used to easily find the best spot for your reading nook. The scale drawing then becomes the blueprint for moving help. Thrilled to see how organized, prepared, and efficient you are—maybe they'll be the ones to buy you pizza!

Fit Activity—Part One of Two

Create a Half-Inch Scale Drawing of a Room

WHAT: Create a drawing that proportionally shrinks any room onto a piece of paper.

WHY: To use as a "fit tool." Predetermine fit of furnishings and accessories according to your vision to eliminate multiple moves by humans.

HOW: Measure the length of the walls, making note of the location of doors, windows, closets, electrical outlets, and heating/cooling vents. Translate those measurements onto a sheet of paper.

TOOLS: Tape measure. Writing utensil (pencil and good eraser encouraged). Paper. Ruler.

TASK:

o Measure the length of each wall, noting windows, location of vents, outlets, door location, and swing direction. See drawings on page 206.

o Convert each wall measurement to inches. A standard ruler scale conversion is one half-inch equals one foot. For example, a ten-by-ten-foot room translates to five-by-five inches on paper.

TIME: Thirty minutes per room.

Translating Feet to Inches

My brother is a double PhD in engineering. Math makes me curl up in a little ball. I panic and nearly cry when faced with simple math. I find converting feet to inches better done on an architectural ruler, a three-sided ruler purchased at an office supply or art store. This ruler will make scale drawing crystal clear.

The architectural ruler does the mathematical work of translating a room to scale. One ruler has over ten different scales. You will likely only use the half inch or quarter inch side of the architectural ruler. If you have a larger room (over sixteen by twenty feet) you'll use the quarter inch scale on the architectural ruler.

The drawing doesn't have to be perfect, but do the best you can to take accurate measurements. Doing so will ensure the right sized furniture will fit properly in the space. A room drawing to scale will look something like this:

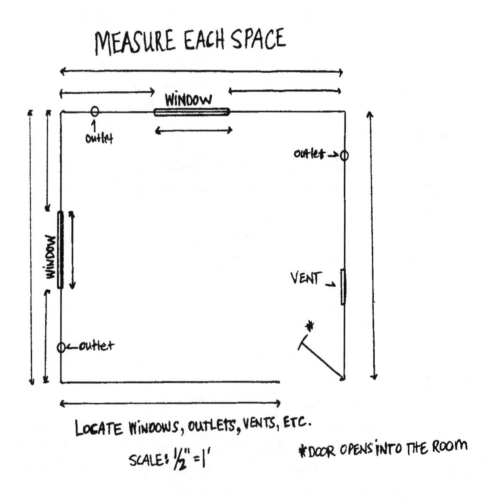

Fit Activity—Part Two of Two

Create Scale Drawings of Large Furniture

WHAT: Create two-dimensional (width and length) representational drawing of your furniture using paper.

WHY: Use to determine fit capabilities within scale drawing of each space.

HOW: Using your architectural ruler, measure the width, length/depth, and height of furniture, and make paper cutouts. See drawings on page 208.

TOOLS: Scissors. Writing utensil (pencil and good eraser encouraged). Paper. Architectural ruler.

TASK:

o   Measure every piece of furniture that will take floor space. Measure the width, depth, and height of each piece. The height of the piece is needed if ceilings, windows, or architectural details will be a factor. You don't want a bookcase in front of a window, for example.

o   Use the same scale used to create the floor plan. Convert furniture measurements to proper scale measurements on paper.

o   Cut out scale drawing of furniture. Place scale furniture on the scale room drawing according to your vision.

o   Label this small piece of paper so you remember which piece of furniture it represents. Include measurements on paper furniture for future use. Save them all in a labeled envelope.

TIME: Thirty minutes per room.

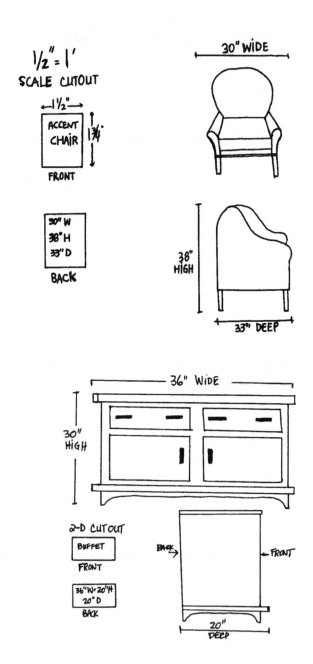

½" = 1'
SCALE CUTOUT

←1½"→
ACCENT CHAIR   1¾"
FRONT

30" W
38" H
33" D
BACK

30" WIDE

38" HIGH

33" DEEP

36" WIDE

30" HIGH

2-D CUTOUT
BUFFET
FRONT

36"W·20"H
20"D
BACK

BACK   FRONT

20" DEEP

Design Your Room

Make magic happen! Place your paper furniture on your paper room. These two together are called a floor plan layout. The floor plan layout is where *your* vision comes alive on paper. You are the designer; your style and the room's function meet. Here are some guidelines:

- Focal point: Is the focus of your room a TV, bed, fireplace, window with a view, or a conversation pit? Place your seating arrangement so it faces the focal point.

- Creature comforts: Does everyone have someplace to set down a beverage? Will you need an occasional guest room? If so, consider a wall bed, a daybed, or a convertible sofa.

- Maximize storage: Use baskets, drawers, and doors in end tables, coffee tables, and ottomans.

- Like with like: Have a clear purpose for each drawer, cabinet, and basket.

- Variety: Vary the size and texture of furniture pieces to create interest.

- Vary the size, color, texture, shape, and material of accessories to create interest.

- Rugs: Area rugs anchor and define a space. Set furniture entirely on the rug, or at least land one under the front legs. Add felt pads to the back legs to create level seating.

- Display and bookcases: If possible, use the entire height of the walls to make the room feel larger. Keep some areas of shelves open. Select a few treasures to display, and arrange books

around those treasures. Use similar baskets or bins throughout the space, when visible, to maintain continuity.

- Lighting: Use for reading and general ambiance to allow safe navigation to, from, and within a space.

Reflection Activity

WHAT: What did you experience as you saw your dream come to life on paper?

: In the space below, answer the reflection question.

_____

_____

_____

_____

_____

_____

_____

_____

Lighting

People often forget about lighting. Proper lighting serves both a practical and aesthetic function. Table and floor lamps create mood, bring light to dark corners, and provide practical lighting for reading and crafting. The type of activities that take place in this space will inform your lighting needs. For example:

- Task lamps: Shine directly on paperwork, reading, writing materials, and keyboards. Under-cabinet lighting or a small lamp illuminates a countertop to ensure safe cutting or chopping in a kitchen or craft area.

- Floor or table lamps: Provide ambient light and mood lighting. They brighten dark corners, making spaces feel warmer and more inviting.

- The bulb: Adds to the function and feel of a space with dimmability and brightness. A bulb's brightness can range, and dimmability allows for a lot of flexibility to create mood or light for any activity in a room.

Examples of Floor Plan Layouts

Fireplace or TV as focal point:
Maximize the view of a fireplace or TV even when placed in a corner. Allow for comfortable walking space through the room and around furnishings (eighteen inches is typical). The console table behind the larger sofa delineates the living space from the walking space. If traffic pattern bisects a room, create two unique spaces (e.g., games, music, etc.).

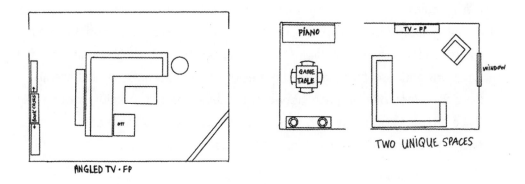

ANGLED TV · FP

TWO UNIQUE SPACES

Rooms with traffic pattern concerns:
Place furniture to best facilitate the traffic flow. Create the best way for people and pets to get from one doorway to the next.

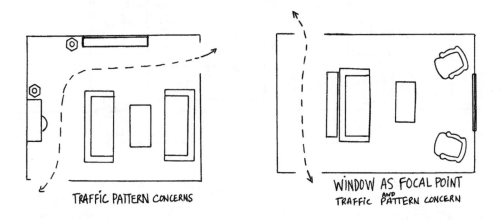

TRAFFIC PATTERN CONCERNS

WINDOW AS FOCAL POINT
TRAFFIC AND PATTERN CONCERN

Long and narrow spaces:
Long and narrow spaces, especially with doors and closets that affect the traffic patterns, can be difficult to furnish. What often helps is to create two separate functional areas within a long narrow space.

Dining rooms:

A dining room buffet is great for storage. Add a mirror over buffets to make the room feel larger. The cabinet on the opposite wall will give that area dual functions and also balance out the weight of the room. Be sure there are at least four feet of clearance between a cabinet and the dining room table. Place a dining room rug two feet from the edge of the table to prevent the back legs of chairs from catching on the rug.

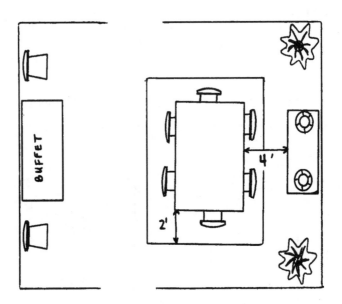

Balance can be achieved by simple placement considerations.

-For walking or traffic zones:

- o Four feet of space is needed to comfortably move people from room to room.

- o Floating furniture in the room away from the walls might allow people to move behind furniture, which could make for a better flow.

-Space between furniture:

- o There should be eighteen inches of space between the edge of a chair or sofa and the edge of a coffee table.

- o Dining chairs should be able to move three feet out from a table.

- o Allow forty-eight inches of space around all sides of a dining table for best serving, seating, and movement.

-TVs: Place TVs at least two or three times their width from seating (e.g., if TV is 50 inches wide, place the TV 150 inches from seating). This rule will also help you purchase the right size TV for the space. Bigger is not always better.

-Bedroom: To get in and out of bed easily, you need twenty-four inches of space between the side of the bed and the wall.

-Make certain all doors can open completely without banging into furniture.

The three Fs, Function, Focus, and Fit, are great tools to dream and think pragmatically about a space. This isn't the sexy side of design but so very essential. The spice and flavor will come next to amp up your vision and your personal style.

Feel

The feel of a space has little to do with the things we touch but rather how the whole space touches our heart. This feeling is a palpable reflection of what makes your life full and meaningful. It can illuminate personal values that embody how we live and express ourselves. Home and style evolve, yet the core essence of who we are is omnipresent.

Loved possessions simply and always convey the heart of who you are. A dining table that is clear except for a loved, whimsical vase from Aunt Yolonda, paired with comfortable chairs from the flea market make this space finally feel right, especially compared to the hard and heavy chairs that used to be there. Your number one treasures happily love you back. Family and friends notice. Home feels like you. You too feel more you.

"The moment you have in your heart this extraordinary thing
called love and feel the depth, the delight, the ecstasy of it,
you will discover that for you the world is transformed."
JIDDU KRISHNAMURTI

Stand back and, once again, look over your possessions. Uncomplicated, simple, classic, natural, modern, eclectic, colorful, spicy, or quirky—these may describe a feeling. Some might call it style. As you or a stranger pass through this space, what feeling, emotions, or words radiate from it? They may come from specific pieces or the whole of the area. Use the space below to capture your thoughts.

Feel and Function

The key is to create a place that functions well, meets users' needs, and expresses character. The quest for the right feel is a journey found in the marriage of function and personality.

- *Comfortable seating*: Generally softer, fuller pieces convey a casual, cozy, and relaxed feel. Firmer, more clean-line pieces read polished, simple, and open. Throw a faux fur blanket on a clean-lined sofa and it too can feel very cozy. Comfort means having the appropriate amount of seating for everyday living and space when needed for additional guests.

- *Walls:* Art, photos, prints, bookcases, and cabinets all add to the feel of a space. Consistency creates more harmony. An eclectic display of color, size, and texture has more energy. Find a tasteful combination of these styles. Stop before it becomes busy or cluttered.

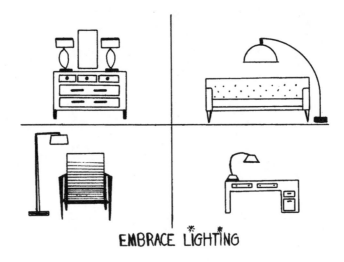

EMBRACE LIGHTING

- *Lighting:* Lighting is critical when creating a mood or conveying a feeling within a space. Daylight or bright overhead light may be necessary for crafting whereas warm light and accent lamps create more intimacy. Experiment with task, accent, and overhead lighting. Switch out the color (lumens) and wattage until the right feel and mood is captured.

- *Include nature:* Green plants, fresh flowers, seashells, twigs, metal sculptures, or rocks add an organic and calm yet connected feel to a space. A wooden bowl can be a perfect place to hold keys by the door.

- *Blankets and pillows:* Pillows and blankets add textures, color, comfort, style, and function to a space. Include grandma's quilt in a cold and drafty space. Fluffy, frilly, sleek, or modern pillows can double as additional seating.

- *Books:* Be selective and intentional about books. Use creativity and restraint. A stack of larger books can become a side table.

Use color of the spines to flavor a space. You can find great ideas on Instagram or Pinterest.

- *Rugs:* Rugs not only add function to keep our toes warm, they connect chairs and sofas or add color to our walls and warmth, artistry, and personality. There are so many styles and patterns that create an elegant or informal feel at all price points. Plush rugs add warmth, while thin-pile rugs with geometric patterns can feel more formal and modern.

- *Window treatments:* Function of window treatments is primarily privacy, yet they also add softness, personality, drama, and warmth to a space. Fancy, complicated window treatments make me nervous. I don't know how to "do" them. Below is an idea that looks hard but it's not too bad and adds softness, interest, and warmth to a room.

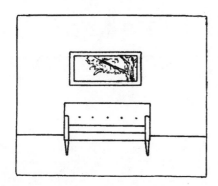 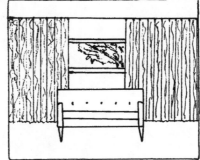

Idea Exploration
Use adjectives that describe your ideal room, then use those words to explore room ideas online or in magazines. For example, is your style funky? Search words like funky, meditative, joyful, and nature-loving by specific room.

Save these ideas in an online or physical folder. Be curious. What spaces reflect you and feel right?

Other ways to be inspired are libraries that hold inspiration in shelved books and magazines. Retail paint supply stores, home furnishing showrooms, family, and friends can be great sources of inspiration. Local colleges or universities have design students who may need a project to work on. Expect good listening skills and an interest to reflect *your* vision and not a current trend or assignment. Your knowing leads the way.

Mini Feel Activity

WHAT: Name three things that represent the feel you want for your space.

1. _____

2. _____

3. _____

WHY: To accomplish your "feel goal."

HOW: Adjust furniture and accessories within your space to achieve your feel goal.

TOOLS: Any existing furniture and accessories.

TASK: Choose one room. Through trial and error create a space that reflects the feelings listed above.

TIME: One hour.

> *"If you never did, you should. These things are fun and fun is good."*
>
> ## DR. SEUSS

Fun

Tap into a sweet, joyful spot of fun. Decluttering is intense, exhausting, puzzling, and effort-filled. Including playfulness and frivolity is much deserved and as Martha Stewart says, "is a good thing." The course work is done. School is out! Let's play.

Play in the form of exploration. Identify objects that symbolize personal passions and values. For example, a lover of nature may find a rock in the shape of an apple or heart as a great addition to a coffee table. If family time is a priority, track down puzzles, playing cards, old photo albums, or board games. Make them accessible in a way that pulls people together. Are meditative or spiritual needs a part of your vision? Enjoy arranging a quiet, cozy, contemplative corner or a benevolent shrine to your source of comfort and strength. Journey through vision creation with unabashed fun.

Fun elicits smiles inside and out. Joyful photos, playing with toys, dancing, old clothes, silly or unique possessions—include anything that doesn't take life too seriously. Below is a mini-activity to conjure what is and has been fun for you.

Fun Memories

My sister introduced me to a Trader Joe's beer called "Simpler Times." I *love* that sentiment so much. Doesn't it just remind you to slow down, look up at the sky, sit on the front stoop, and watch the wind gently move through outstretched branches? I feel my worry shift, feel carefree, and unfurrow the deep crease between my brows.

Remember your simpler times. Times without angst, obligation, and stress. The carefree meanderings, spontaneous time with friends or family that led to a picnic, or simply a nap in the middle of the day. Something about simple things holds such joy.

Indulge in a bit of fun each day until fun becomes a habit again. Below are some questions to reconnect with fun. Questions are like Life Savers candy. Take a piece of "candy" from the list below, and savor it on a train ride, walk, or while doing dishes.

- What are your funniest memories from childhood?

- Who was fun to play with? Today?

- What qualities are consistent in these fun friends?

- What occasions are fun and why?

- Notice fun or funny things today.

Write each fun or funny thing down on a piece of paper, and place it in a bowl. Pull one out every now and again, and see how your mood and the day changes. Think of fun like fairy dust, creating an element of surprise.

Music is often forgotten and yet is so magical. Songs that make you dance and smile, like polka music (just hop a lot), "The Chicken Dance," songs from your childhood, and current music that moves your spirit all add fun. I have included music throughout the book to touch your heart and soul and connect to each chapter musically. My hope is that it adds a spark of fun too.

Stored heirloom linens pulled out of drawers can become wall art. Unused barnwood made into frames comes alive and holds family photos. Rope lights tacked to the bottom of a sofa or frame of a doorway can add a touch of surprise to a room. Light those long-ignored candles. Wrap sculptures in ribbons, sunglasses, or a scarf. Toss a furry red pillow on a bed. Bake and display a tray of fresh cookies in the kitchen (they won't last long!). Create a funny bone section in the "Style File." Decide to revive well-deserved fun-filled spaces.

Vision Actualized Starts Here

After familiarizing yourself with these five design tools, now is the time to put them to work to actualize your vision.

FUNCTION → FOCUS → FIT → FEEL → FUN !

I hope your instinct is to create a plan because that is exactly what needs to be done to actualize your vision. As in all prior projects, first determine the scope of work. Brainstorm, as before, your project list, included below. The scope is a list of rooms, spaces, and places to design. Use what you have to re-design loved and needed things (furniture and accessories) to reveal your vision.

VISION ACTUALIZED PROJECT LIST	
Room/Space	Project & Goal
1.	
2.	
3.	
4.	
5.	

Next, prioritize the vision project list. Use the questions below to help flesh out your priorities.

- What space is manageable as a place to begin?

- Where are you eager to see results?

- Where do you *live* the most?

- Where do you live in the least? This might be a great place to practice your vision.

- Where does an urgent need surface (sleep, meals, entertaining, laundry, etc.) as critical?

- Where can you be most successful?

- What project is closely linked to your values?

- What project most feeds your vision?

Focus on one space at a time to safeguard against frustration and paralysis.

As a starting point, in the space below, write down your top three vision projects.

VISION ACTUALIZED PRIORITY LIST		
Room or Area	Priority	Completed

A blank canvas is easiest to work from. If possible, consider removing everything from the room and rebuilding it from the ground up. I realize this approach may not be doable. At minimum, remove items that will not have a home in the space you are working in.

With each project, practice each design principle one at a time. You may be excited to get in and mess with everything, but be patient. Like any new skill, the road is lumpy at first. Over time, understanding and comfort level of the concepts, goals, and disciplines of the five principles will increase. Some principles will be easier to grasp and implement than others. Use your creative spirit to become the designer of *your* vision. Picking and choosing a few tips in each principle is enough to shift the way you look and react to your space.

Consult your floor plan layout. Add furnishings in layers. Start with larger pieces of furniture, otherwise known as the anchors of the space, like the sofa, bed, dining table, larger wall art, buffet, or dressers. Slowly sprinkle in the secondary items, like smaller storage pieces, chairs, or side tables. Adjust and arrange one piece at a time. The accessories—lamps, knick-knacks, pillows, smaller wall hangings—are the sprinkles on the ice cream, adding color, texture, and personality.

At each layer, as loved and needed items enter the room, ask, "How does this space feel now?" Pay attention to the tipping point when furniture is too big or there is too much in a space. Stop adding just before the space feels "full."

Always keep refining. Let go of anything that is clouding or crowding your vision.

Tips to help move through the visioning process:

- Put "like" things together in *one* location. Keep blankets, books, remotes, magazines, utensils, etc. all together in one spot. Everything has a place. Everything in its place.

- Move less frequently used possessions to less valuable space.

- Ensure easy access to often-used items. Stick to a "grab and go" efficiency.

- Commit to 100 percent visibility of things in each drawer, basket, or on each shelf. Avoid things behind books or under beds if possible. Visibility is key.

- Rearrange, remove, and reprioritize possessions until everything is in the right place.

- Unsure where something fits? Ask, "If this was in the perfect, most obvious location, where would this piece fit?"

- Be flexible: a coat closet might make a great office or games closet.

- Associate and connect things: if a fireplace is associated with reading or games, put those possessions by the fireplace. If bill paying is associated with the kitchen, place associated possessions in the kitchen.

As discernment blossoms, it becomes easier and easier to recognize what works. Maintain a willingness to try new things, and don't run away, but pivot if problems arise. The resilience you gained resides within. Patience is rewarded with perseverance. Keep moving. When your space is right, you will feel an exhale of relief. Take in *your* loved space. Congrats, courageous one.

"Dream lofty dreams, and as you dream, so shall you become. Your Vision is the promise of what you shall one day be. Your Ideal is the prophecy of what you shall at last unveil."

JAMES ALLEN

The power to create your perfect home lies within you. What you desire is possible and within your control. It's not the size of the space that is significant, it is how you make that space reflect the you-ness of you. Love, nurture, and have a full life in this space forever and ever. Amen.

"Into the Mystic"
Gretchen Wilson

9 | Healthy Habits. Healthy Home.

*"Discipline is choosing between what you want
now and what you want most."*
ABRAHAM LINCOLN

Diving into one concept, one chapter at a time was intentional. My hope was the pace allowed you an opportunity to soak up sometimes weighty information. Concentrate on one facet of yourself and the role that clutter plays to help you chart a healthier relationship with your home one concept at a time. Allow incremental bits of mental and emotional stamina to buoy you as you swim through the waves decluttering can bring. I imagine you coming out of the cluttered cave, throwing your arms in the air, absorbing the warm sun, undeterred, able to confront clutter, prepared to live fully in a home you made real.

Now that we are nearing the end of this journey, what is different within you and your space from page one to now? How has your perspective on excess changed? How has your space been altered? Remember what you hoped would happen as a result of this working journal. Return to the introduction to reflect on what you set out to achieve reading this book. The reflection activity below can help flush out your thoughts.

Reflection Activity: *Measure Your Progress*

WHAT: What cluttered space, behavior, or feeling in your space(s) did you change as a result of this working journal?

WHY: To measure your progress against your intentions from the introduction.

HOW: Measure your satisfaction with all decluttering goals you intended.

TOOLS: One sheet of paper and a writing utensil, computer or tablet.

TASK: Rate your satisfaction, from one to ten, with one being extremely dissatisfied and ten being extremely satisfied with reaching the clutter management goal you made at the beginning of the book.

TIME: Thirty minutes.

Reflection Activity

WHAT: What is one thing you would do differently?

: In the space below, answer the reflection question.

_____

_____

_____

_____

_____

_____

_____

How much have you changed your thoughts and behaviors around clutter? How engaged were you with your decluttering goals? Rate from one to ten, with one being "very little" and ten being "extremely."

What worked? How will you challenge yourself to be more engaged?

Hey, this is a difficult process. It's OK to miss the mark. Know that wherever you are is perfect. Don't give up. Notice small positive changes you've made. Recognize any new behaviors you have incorporated. Everything you do to dominate clutter matters. Any effort big or small has the potential to be an inflection point, an ember that could restart a clutter-free revolution. Believe it could happen. I won't give up on you. Don't give up on yourself.

Always celebrate any amount of clutter movement and improvement. Did you recycle the newspaper or magazine before the next one came? Did you put the pencil back in the pencil holder, or fold and put away the laundry in the same day? These small actions will get you closer to your actualized loved home. Please don't give up hope or effort. Take stock in ideas that seemed plausible and sustainable. Take inventory of areas of interest and enthusiasm.

Maintain Clutter Management Momentum

Capturing impactful moments after seeing a stirring movie, concert, or live theater event is exhilarating. Collecting inner awakenings from any part of this book is invaluable. I am not comparing this working journal to seeing the *Lion King* live in all its majesty. However, I hope you learned at least one new technique and changed one behavior to conquer clutter long-term. My hope is one spark of motivation leads to one new decluttering behavior. Everything you do matters.

Reflect on each chapter. If you took notes or highlighted ideas, list those "light bulb" revelations on a single sheet of paper, or on your computer or tablet. Create your own CliffsNotes version of ideas that resonated. Mine for everything that spurred hope, possibility, or ideas. Use these as sparks of motivation and reminders to continue to chase clutter out the door. Your takeaways are as unique as you are.

Values in Action

You are here because senseless acquisition doesn't complete you. Know what you stand for. Wear your values like a coat of arms. Write your top three values on your hand or tape them to your wallet and credit cards. Get these ideals up in your grill. *You* are in control. Use your values as a snare and silence the madness around you.

Create visual reminders of these values on sticky notes in prominent places. Embody these values. Exemplify one value each month. Experience a concentrated dose of what fills you. Add time in your calendar to prioritize values. Take a walk, nature lover. Go to church, community seeker. Phone a relative, family maker. Lifelong learner, read from all those unread books already in your possession.

Deliberately incorporate ways to encompass each value each month. See all these life-giving experiences as gifts, not extravagances. Go on a quest to live those beautiful personal values. Heed that urging from your truest self to keep living fully in a loved and sacrosanct space.

Vision Out Front

Keep your vision in sight. Your vision is your light, fire, and hope. Display your vision front and center, as a focal point on the wallpaper on your phone or computer screen or on a prominent wall or door you pass by daily. Each encounter with your vision board produces little floating "possibility bubbles" into the universe, working with you to make real your dream home. I promise your desired changes will manifest, if they haven't already because of the wonder twin powers: doing the work of decluttering and the universe calling your dreams into reality.

Choosing

The means to your vision is through the valley of choices. There is no way around you making choices. Every positive decluttering choice you make, day in and day out, lightens the load and makes the journey to your vision easier. Know which choice methods worked best for you. Feel free to make up unique ways of letting go of excess. Declare "Move It Mondays," or "Tear through It Tuesdays." Find unique (and safe) ways to stay engaged and have fun decluttering.

Dismantle. Disperse.

As long as you consume goods, dismantle and disperse are necessary. Moving things in, out of, and within your dwelling will never go away. Don't let your guard down. It's healthy to address complacency. We don't always know when or where we have gotten stuck with excess stuff. Build in an anti-clutter plan. Every six months throw a real or imaginary bash. Get ready for a houseful of your closest friends. Look at your space from the eyes of the person you admire most. Use this anti-clutter plan to challenge a pile or a process that has crept into your life and home.

As a consumer, stuff is constant. Excess often goes unnoticed until it gets out of hand. When life gets too busy to manage excess, it's time to create a project list and get to work. Go through drawers and closets regularly. Is everything in the right place? Be in pursuit of the best place for and the right amount of XYZ. Evaluate the many piles of like items to ensure what you own is loved and needed and little more. Dismantle and disperse diligently.

Giving

You are a giver of love, time, and care. Continue to be a giver of things. Doing so completes the decluttering cycle. An approachable giving plan is foundational. Strive to create a plan that is as clear and as effortless as possible. A donation bin is your eternal and faithful friend that never leaves your side. So much so that giving away and letting go of excess becomes an essential expression of a most full and rich life.

Vision Actualized

The reason we are here is to get you home. I am so proud of every ounce of willingness you brought to the table. The results of your work are magnificent. The motivation to do this work, to create a loved home, grew from the inside of you! *You* dared to deviate from old ways of doing and believing. No matter where you are on this journey, what you have accomplished is incredible.

This glow coming from your home is not just your radiant actualized vision; it is the embodiment of your beautiful soul. This space, as well as you, will continue to transform and develop more stillness. Tranquility will come from having less clutter, stress, and anxiety and more time to savor the present. You're living with the truest parts of who you are in a place you love. Home.

Growing Healthy Habits

I hope how you see your life and your home has been altered forever. You've made many positive, consistent changes. Ultimately, you're forming many new effective and realistic habits. These small, steady steps of change to master your messes are necessary and energizing. How does that happen? By planning and doing.

Plan and Work Your Plan

Whatever you do, have a plan. Proactively prepare a plan today for what needs to be done tomorrow. Imagine in what circumstances you will be vulnerable to making poor choices. The diet analogy is helpful once again. Prepare for the big beautiful retail buffet of excess that is right at your fingertips and out your front door. Avoid being ambushed by complacency, and come prepared to manage temptations.

Be on alert. Avoid being caught off guard. In advance, look at your schedule days or weeks ahead. Highlight situations where you have been or might be tempted to acquire stuff. Take charge of the situation and create a plan. Brainstorm ways to avoid buying unnecessary things. Don't bring a credit card or only bring X amount of cash. Come up with creative excuses. You don't want to carry it, don't have room for it, don't collect that stuff anymore.

Don't be afraid to change your schedule. Depending on how confident you feel, suggest doing something less tempting. If you go to the event, plan to allow yourself one reasonable indulgence. Set limits and stick to the plan.

Triggers

Know your triggers. Be it sales, certain stores, impulse buys, online shopping, or shopping with friends or family. Yes, you can just walk away, shut off the computer, and avoid temptation entirely, but this tactic isn't possible long-term. Is it a grocery shopping day, weekend warrior shopping, family celebrations, or a holiday that makes you over shop? What will you encounter that will trigger potential zombie shopping? Take control and mitigate mindless or obsessive gathering of goods.

If you can't find the exact thing you intended to buy, don't buy it. Restrain the urge to bring home another "almost right." If you do buy an "almost right" it doesn't mean you have to keep it. Always get a copy of the store's return policy. Even when you have made thoughtful purchases, it doesn't mean you have to keep them. When you bring something new home, take time within the return policy to evaluate what you hoped to happen and what actually happened when you got the piece home. Does it serve the purpose you hoped? Do you love it? Is the item vital? If not, return it.

Value limit-setting. How will you hold yourself accountable next time to honor this sacred home? There will always be temptations. Over time you will bank enough successes to deal with enticements.

Eye on the Prize

Moving through the day-to-day is like looking down while you are hiking. You just plow ahead and forget to pull your head up. When you do, you see the magnificence on the horizon. Keep looking up! Remember the reason you are doing all of this decluttering. Keep your vision top of mind. Photograph your vision board so it's available to you anytime you need a reminder. You and your vision are a team navigating through all the clutter in the world. Together you know what is needed and avoid being sold something you don't need or want. Your vision won't settle and neither should you.

Remember, patience builds much-needed resilience. Allow the universe to bring you what you need. Trust. It will appear in due time. I wanted outdoor side tables for my small deck. I wanted them to have thin black metal bases to match the railing, and I wanted them to be a certain height, round, sturdy, yet easy to move and big enough to hold a beverage and a dinner plate. I also wanted them to be accented with lime green. Hard to find, right?

I looked at a dozen websites and saw a lot of "almost" side tables. I remained firmly determined and full of trust that this needle in a haystack would show up. A few weeks later, I found the side table on Target's website. I spray painted the wooden top lime green and boom—the rest is history, until the wood tops warped because I didn't use marine-grade paint. So I found clay pot bases that fit perfectly and spray painted them lime green. I have so many personal examples where my vision, the universe, and patience have helped me find what was missing. Tap in. There is a lot of this mojo to go around.

Maintaining Healthy Habits

I hope this powerful and profound decision to tackle clutter ignites an eternally burning desire to stay ahead of messes. No one alive is immune to consuming. We have to eat, clothe ourselves, and sleep, all within a safe space, making us all vulnerable to recklessness. Even when the space you love feels totally complete, consumerism still confronts, swarming us daily. Managing our possessions is a forever thing. Decisions just get easier to make.

Manage Clutter Creep

Setting limits never takes a vacation. Notice when clutter is forming. Tolerating things being left in certain places at certain times is normal. Set a timeline for items that belong elsewhere to find their true home. I notice these things happening in large retail stores. Toothpaste is left in the pasta aisle. Adult socks are found with the kids' toys. I have to think there was an emergency and the shopper had to leave quickly. Someone has to come by and return those items to their rightful place. You become that someone in your own home.

Designate time each day or every few days to collect and distribute left items to their rightful homes.

The following activity will encourage you to manage your clutter from this day forward.

Activity #1: Clutter Creep Management Plan

Conscious clutter awareness is necessary forever. Clutter creeps in, first unseen, then one day it's back again and overwhelming. Stop its insidious encroachment.

WHAT: Create a plan to mindfully remove excess.

WHY: You are ultimately responsible for clutter management of your spaces.

HOW: Manage clutter creep: Pay attention. Change your behaviors. Hold yourself accountable.

TOOLS: Calendar (phone or hard copy), writing utensil, computer or tablet, accountability partner.

TASK: Create two ways you will manage clutter. Ideas:

o   Set calendar appointments.

o   Mindfully monitor. Take a photo of ideal space and again at week's end. Adjust behaviors accordingly.

o   Donate "to-go" items every three months.

o   Clear surfaces one set day each week.

o   Invite people over.

o   Have an accountability partner with whom you exchange weekly photo or video check-ins.

TIME: As needed.

Reflection Activity

WHAT: What two clutter management tools will you incorporate?

: In the space below, answer the reflection question.

Like with Like

The beauty of this concept is proximity keeps you honest. If every like thing is together, you know how much you have. Four places for socks and you'll have four times the socks you need. All the sheets are in the linen closet. All the everyday and the good glassware is in its respective cabinet. Excess toilet paper goes in one closet. Like with like. Safeguard this tight rule. Protect your boundaries here at all cost. Migration into other areas is a surefire collapse of clutter control.

New In

By now, even before you open your wallet, always ask yourself two questions: Is this thing a need or want? Secondly, is there a place and space for it to live comfortably? Answer with crystal clarity. If you can't answer either of these questions, shut your wallet. Go home and do your research.

New in at no cost doesn't fly. The cost to bring in something new is an old one needs to come out. One for one. One old out pays for one new in. Have a plan to remove something prior to purchasing.

Beware of Storage Bins

Plastic is magnificent yet menacing. The list of how plastics are used could fill every page of this book. The one I want to talk about is the storage bin. For clutter, it is one piece of plastic that is both a blessing and a curse. It's great for getting those like items together, such as seasonal décor, memorabilia, or art supplies. With beautiful clear labeling, they get tucked away until they are called upon to be used.

The storage bin becomes the "Son of Satan" (say with a menacing voice) when stuff is locked up in these clutter coffins. This stuff often never comes out, and never gets used for years and years and years. I could go on. Just the other day I removed five storage bins of home décor used in a prior home a year ago. Will we use it in our new home? Turns out, 90 percent of the contents went straight to my local preferred donation site. Off it went into someone else's home, cabin, or whatnot. Each holiday is an opportunity to declutter this type of décor.

Proactively set a limit for the number of storage bins you keep. Schedule time to go through each bin every six months. Storage bins are an active part of your possessions, not a place where things go to die. Set an "all storage bin review" soon, then schedule another date six months out. Memorabilia is not off the hook. Find ways to make letting go that much easier. Put photos in digital formats. Pull things out of these bins to use or enjoy. When things come out of hiding, often the luster wears off of the item, and you discover the memory is enough. Select the few pieces of baby clothes that hold the most memories. Make a blanket and donate the rest. Confront excess continuously. Consciously and keenly hone the choices you make every day. You are always refining. Refine. Refine. Refine.

New Ways to Celebrate

Prognosticate on how post-decluttering celebrations will look. Most likely, your ways of celebrating in the past will look different today. Less stuff, I hope. If it's not about the stuff anymore, then what? Certain parts of those events held the meaning. My guess is it isn't the gifts. What is the essence of being together you love the most? What are you most grateful for?

Warm-Up Exercise

WHAT: Besides gifts, take inventory of what you love about celebrations.

WHY: To divert focus from "things" to the people you love and care about.

HOW: Analyze one or two typical group celebrations.

TOOLS: Writing utensil and paper or computer or tablet.

TASK: List one or two loved group celebrations. List all events, feelings, and emotions that give each celebration meaning for you.

TIME: Thirty minutes.

Reflection Activity

WHAT: How will you reduce the emphasis of stuff at your next celebration?

: In the space below, answer the reflection question.

_____

_____

_____

_____

_____

_____

_____

_____

Traditions don't change easily. You are one person, but little by little you can share this new direction with those you love and trust. People find comfort in tradition and routine, and not everyone will honor this change. Respect those who aren't ready to change. Often, if you are joyful and consistent about your new perspective, a new tradition can grow.

Reorganize to Reenergize

During the pandemic we were all home, and many of us were living close together in the same space for a long time and not spending money on travel. A lot of issues surfaced regarding our home's efficiencies and comfort. Offices needed to be created as more people worked and went to school virtually. More privacy was needed while in the house, and outdoor living environments expanded.

Before the pandemic, furnishings were set in place and rarely moved. Hopefully the decluttering process made you more comfortable to look at your spaces with opportunistic eyes. Don't be afraid to move stuff around!

My mother has always been a big proponent of moving our living room furniture every few months. Sofa, chairs, and accent tables would be slid this way and that. Lamps shifted, wall hangings were rearranged, a once used blanket was tossed over the arm of the sofa, and just like that, the place looked new. I thought it was pretty cool to come home to what felt like a new house. We didn't have a lot of money to buy new furniture, but it didn't keep Mom from creating a new mood. Popping home to this change in perspective sparked both a thrill and a lot of pride for my mom.

What my mom did is now called redesigning. Redesigning is using furnishings in new and different ways. If you have an itch for newness that needs to be scratched, stop and assess the problem that needs to be solved. Are you bored and craving something new? Is the space inefficient, causing frustration? What is not feeling, looking, or working right? Once the problem is clearly identified, go on a hunt *within* your four walls to solve the problem.

For example:

Problem	Possible Solution
Bored. Need something new?	- Move large furnishings to a new location. - Switch accent pillows from one room to another. - Remove everything from a shelf or bookcase. Reintroduce new items. - Paint a room, a wall, a flowerpot, or a chair. - Transplant plants into different containers. - Hang a rug as wall art. Move rugs around. - Add or replace a tablecloth. - Bring something from nature inside. Rock. Branch. Pinecones. - Cluster several candles or a variety of vases together. - Remove something. - Switch out or cluster photos in frames. Cluster framed art on walls.
Solve seating issues	- Rest pillows under coffee table. Use it as a game table. - Tie two pillows together like a present for floor seating. - Place pillows on top of coffee table as seating. - Hide small stools under coffee table. - Replace fabric on chairs.
Manage games or crafts	- Inside storage ottomans, in cabinets, or drawers. - Store in suitcases in closet or under bed. - Put up hooks behind doors to hold bag of games, crafts, etc.

The goal is to resist the knee-jerk reaction to add new stuff. Go online with your problem. Look for frugal, in-home solutions first.

Another option is to repurpose things to create something new. Be willing to look at, use, or transform furnishings or accessories to be used in a new way. If you have a chest of drawers but need a kitchen island, there is a way to repurpose the chest of drawers. Headboard and footboard into a bench. An outdoor garden bench into a planter. I have seen a garden rake turned into a wine glass holder. Surprises and new perspectives await your creative redesigns. Redesigning and repurposing are incredible instruments of change to creatively beautify and make your home function as needs change.

Desire Undeterred

For me, growing up in a small suburb of St. Paul, Minnesota, was predictable. I had parents who went out for the New Year's dance, highly anticipated easy summers of active sports, motocross races, mindless meandering, school, church, holidays with relatives, family dinners, and a week each summer on Pelican Lake. Repeated annually for ten years.

All of us kids were told we had to go to college and how we got there was up to us. No complaints really, until the end of my freshman year at a local college. The things I enjoyed at college consisted of my ping-pong-playing roommate Bridget, my freedom, and learning about God. When Bridget told me she wasn't coming back the next year, my concept of the world imploded. What? Change course? Because you want to? What?! Wait, change is possible? I was paying for my college, so if she could leave and do what she wanted, so could I.

This revelation blew open my secret desire to go to a college in the mountains. In high school I had taken trips with friends to Colorado, Montana, and Wyoming. I could rearrange my life! I told my parents I was going to go to another school. Far, far away. They responded, "Why do you want to do that? There are perfectly good schools nearby." I can't explain it, but I was undeterred. I went back to my high school counselor's office and straight to the Colorado section, and pulled out a mountain-filled catalog for a small college in Durango, Colorado. That summer, I applied, was accepted, and left before my parents adjusted to what was happening.

My desire for adventure was unleashed. I found a job, a roommate, independence, possibility, confidence, and empowerment. My hope is you too can break through unknown barriers and alter forever what you knew was possible. This internal knowing is in all of us. Do you hold an ember inside you that needs a little fanning? Whisper it in my ear. I will hold your dream. Now that you mentioned it out loud, the universe heard you too. I can't wait to see what happens.

Transformation

You're learning new skills, like how to choose, eliminate, move, and organize stuff, and training yourself to be a project manager and home designer, able to marinate on questions, engage with activities, craft project plans, establish priorities, and do the hard work that once looked as daunting as traversing the Grand Canyon. The preparation, sweat, time, and the doing of decluttering can press heavy on the mind, body, and soul. But you have faced resistance and doubt, and recognized no one will get you to the top of the canyon—or the home you love—but you. This decluttering process is arduous, but it's also manageable *and* incredibly liberating.

All of this mental and emotional work is fueled by immeasurable bravery. Eventually, internal transformation will replace those old fears. Wires in the brain will untie old beliefs and solder new pathways of doing things. Freshly unlocked resilience, forgiveness, and tenderness will allow for change to occur more easily. All of these are beautiful byproducts of traversing through the landscape of messes. The creation of a loved abode is worth persevering through every hard thing. Who cares if you approach this journey with the enthusiasm of a kid on a slip-n-slide or reluctantly sticking a toe in the rushing creek? Both are worthy of a bravery badge.

Journey

Over time, the journey from subtly noticing chaos becomes an "I've had enough!" raucous revolt. Excess as a problem and addressing that problem is different for everyone. Years are most often needed between recognizing you are stuck, deciding to get unstuck, and actually becoming unstuck. We've all been stuck. Stuck in traffic. Stuck in a bad relationship. Stuck between a rock and a hard place. Make a decision to get unstuck.

I believe, to do the work and make meaningful change, you have to start from the inside. Understand where your clutter and your soul are jammed up. Acceptance is also your launching pad.

The internal and physical work of decluttering takes time, energy, and focus over long quiet walks, mini meditations, or *ahas* in random places with friends, family, or hired help. And you did it. I just put words on paper. I have learned you cannot pull anyone along in this process. I am certain you bumped up against so many challenges, persevered through tough stuff, and discovered a pace that felt right for you. *You* did all of this training. You ran the marathon. *You* are awe inspiring!

"Life is a circle. The end of one journey is the beginning of the next."
JOSEPH M. MARSHALL III

Journey is about passage and moving from one stage of life to another. It's about learning to loosen our control over some areas and ask for help in others. Go forth, wherever you are, my friend, because this journey through clutter to your one big life is worth it. Lead, take charge, and enjoy your hard-won freedom.

Working with a Home Coach

As a life coach, I have the privilege and opportunity to develop my own unique niche. You can be a life coach who focuses on career coaching, health coaching, or executive coaching to name just a few. I have chosen to bring what I have learned about creating a home into a unique niche of helping people love their homes. It so happens that 100 percent of my coaching clients love their home after decluttering. I help clients look at everything within and about their home from a new perspective.

By asking curious questions, the home coach awakens the client to new insights that often unlock old habits and create movement and improvement in the way one lives and moves within their living space. The goal is to help them understand and love themselves more while living with less. If one can do this on their own, they do not need a home coach. If not, this home coach is here to help.

The benefits of hiring a home coach are to help:

- Identify goals, dreams, and vision you have for a loved home

- Identify barriers to those goals and dreams

- Prioritize removal of all roadblocks

- Develop a decluttering team

- Create accountability to the doing of decluttering

- Encourage, re-engage through inaction, motivate, remind, observe, support through every stage of decluttering

- Move the client through every stage of the life-giving decluttering process until the goal, dream, and vision for a loved home are achieved

-   Repeat if needed

Your home coach will not give up on you or your dreams, goals, and vision. Together the coach and client form an alliance where every effort to create or alter movement toward the client's goals is priority one. The coach will remind the client of their values and goals when motivation and momentum become stagnant. The coach holds the client as capable, competent, and creative to solve any problem that stands in the way of creating the home they love. The coach has only the best interest of the client.

Do you need a home coach? When you have decluttered time and time again and you end up in the same pile of stuff, this would be a great time to hire a home coach. There can be a lot of starts and stops to the decluttering process, and if you feel like you never finish, that may be an indication it's time to hire a home coach. When you have been saying, "I need to get rid of stuff," over and over again for years, it is time to hire a home coach. When you have given up hope of ever living in a home you love, that is a great time to hire a home coach.

If someone tells you to hire a home coach and you resent it or disagree, this is *not* a good time to hire a home coach. Come with a willing heart to the decluttering party. You have to *want* to do this work, even a little, and you will make a change. With the help of a home coach, family, and friends, use this book to create a supportive community to help one another through the decluttering process.

Well-being in one's home leads to well-being toward others. As a home coach, I model this well-being. I pledge to honor and support the beliefs, values, individuality, objectives, and goals of my clients so they can grow and expand their personal and/or professional lives.

When you hire a home coach or any coach, remember these important guidelines:

- You deserve respect for your individual requirements, limitations, and personal boundaries.

- You deserve to receive constructive and instrumental feedback and have your well-being and expressed desires put first.

- You deserve to expect the coach's own self-interest or personal gain will not surpass your best interests.

- You deserve to establish a mature, respectful, and reasonable relationship that is mutually reciprocated.

- You deserve to feel confident that any work or information about you—the client—is confidential and is not shared without your express permission.

- You deserve to expect that guidance, advice, and counsel will be offered only in areas of your coach's expertise.

- You deserve mutually agreeable terms in the event you need to terminate the working relationship with your coach.

Your coach should also pledge to continually pursue their development as a professional coach by making a commitment to their own personal growth and exploration, maintaining a connection to the coaching community at large by meeting regularly with peers, leaders, and educators.

Activity #2: Day One vs. Now

WHAT: Conduct a personal assessment. Who were you on day one and how do you compare to the person you are today as a result of the decluttering work you did?

WHY: To articulate changes. To acknowledge and celebrate your growth.

HOW: Review the first chapter of the book. Review this last chapter.

TOOLS: Writing utensil and paper, or computer or tablet.

TASK: Write a short paragraph that outlines how you have changed during this journey.

TIME: Fifteen minutes.

Reflection Activity

WHAT: How will you celebrate and share what you have learned?

In the space below, answer the reflection question.

_____

_____

_____

_____

_____

_____

_____

_____

Activity #3: Less Is More

WHAT: What have you gained by having less?

WHY: To anchor the benefit of living with less.

HOW: Explain what "Less is more" means to you.

TOOLS: Writing utensil and paper, or computer or tablet.

TASK: Write a letter to yourself, the person who embarked on this journey. Express what it feels like to live with less today.

TIME: Twenty minutes.

Reflection Activity

WHAT: Find one item, spot, room, or word to summarize your transformation.

: In the space below, answer the reflection question.

_____

_____

_____

_____

_____

_____

_____

_____

> *"The most difficult thing is the decision to act. The rest is merely tenacity."*
> **AMELIA EARHART**

Wherever you are on this journey, don't give up. Stay vigilant. Maintain clutter-free momentum and habits. Acknowledge your tenacity. Believe in your dream. I stand with you, beaming with pride and admiration. Remain forever observant and vigilant.

♩

"Here I Am"
Dolly Parton

Acknowledgments

Over the ten-plus years it took me to write this book, whenever I was asked what I was doing, I would say I was writing a book to help people love their home and manage excess using values, vision, and compassion. Every person I told would inevitably mention that they themselves, or someone they knew, needed to read this book. Every one of you encouraged me to get back on the horse and to press on. Thank you.

To my wife, my love and perpetually positive partner, thank you for your support as I avoided, abhorred, and was energized by this book. At times you booted me back into writing when life's "critical" distractions led me astray.

Thank you to my friends and family for listening, asking (or kindly not asking), and ultimately supporting me through the many phases of my life and this book. To the one and only Mary Jane B. You are the best parts of this book.

I want to thank my editors—Connie Anderson of Words and Deeds, Inc.; Diane Keyes, friend and author of *This Sold House;* Snoop Sista (AKA Cindy D); and Alyssa Bluhm and Emily Krempholtz of Wise Ink Creative Publishing team—including a big thanks to Dara Beevas for seeing my vision and giving me a title that captured my intention. To all of you, your clear, precise, and constructive approach to my writing made me feel like a real writer. As promised, you made me fall in love with my book again. Priceless!